Motivational Ideas for Changing Lives

981

MOTIVATIONAL IDEAS FOR CHANGING LIVES

Neil E. Jackson, Jr.

BROADMAN PRESS
Nashville, Tennessee

© Copyright 1982 • Broadman Press.
All rights reserved.
4256-47
ISBN: 0-8054-5647-3
Dewey Decimal Classification: 248.5
Subject heading: WITNESSING
Library of Congress Catalog Card Number: 81-68366
Printed in the United States of America

Dedication

To *Dr. Rel Gray,* who gave me my start in Southern Baptist work, as his associate pastor in northwest Arkansas, 1954. Just becoming a Southern Baptist, I knew nothing about a Sunday School organization. He introduced me to the study course system and said, "When you get an idea, try it. If it works, use it. If it doesn't, forget it, but keep on reading." That year I read seventy study course books—my immediate education to do the job.

To *Dr. Edgar Williamson,* former Arkansas state Sunday School director, who gave me my start in denominational programming, 1956. He taught me the fundamentals of organizing and building a growing church. He said, "Neil, in programming for a growing church, make four things priority: enrollment, standards, training, and visitation. If you do this, you will have a growing church."

To *Dr. J. D. Grey,* pastor emeritus of First Baptist Church, New Orleans, who taught me the basics in administration, planning, and promotion, 1960. He said, "Neil, make sure your 'ducks are in a row' before you make a presentation. When you get an idea, put it on paper. Put it in your desk for a day or two, take it out, add, delete, change to strengthen. Put it back in the desk. Follow the same process until you are satisfied with the idea. If you can't put your ideas on paper, you will not be able to communicate them to people. *Think* promotion. Nothing will happen unless it is promoted."

These men had their unique input in my life. Two have died. One is retired. *Their* ideals continue through me and now to you as you read.

Foreword

I know of no more enthusiastic person involved in doing the work of the Lord in the ministry of education than Neil Jackson. His warmth and ebullience are accompanied by a sound experiential base for a sharing of ideas on motivation. Since motivation without concomitant action rings as false as the noisy gong and clanging cymbal Paul talks about, it is heartening to observe that Neil can not only prescribe for some of the rest of us—he has taken his own medicine. He exemplifies in his vocation and avocations the highly motivated life changer.

No author, editor, publisher, or foreword writer ought to make guarantees—even limited ones—for "how-to" books. Yet the principles in *Motivational Ideas for Changing Lives* are practical, and the Master's followers can surely claim the guarantees expressed in the New Testament.

In this book, Neil leaves little to chance. He lays the motivational foundation and follows through with practical application blueprints to enhance the growth experience of the seeking reader and maximize the growth results in the churches.

GRADY C. COTHEN
President
The Sunday School Board of the Southern Baptist Convention

Introduction

Motivational Ideas for Changing Lives is an excellent title for Neil Jackson's book. It is full of ideas and is strongly motivational. Its ideas will help to change lives. Some ideas you will choose to use—some you will choose not to use. The author suggests that himself.

Neil Jackson, the man, is energetic, enthusiastic, involved, and creative. He is full of ideas. His book is like that. It moves with force and vigor, and is filled with creativity. Neil is experienced. He has served twelve years in the local church and with The Sunday School Board of the Southern Baptist Convention since 1963. He has traveled across the nation, speaking in associations, churches, and conventions. His book reflects this experience. It is practical, workable, usable.

I believe this book will help pastors, ministers of education, Sunday School directors, Sunday School teachers, and Sunday School class officers and members. I believe it will help them in reaching men and women, boys and girls for Christ and his church. I believe also that this is a book which contains information and help for those who seek to assist the local church in carrying out the Commission our Lord has given it. I believe the book catches the spirit and speaks in a practical way to many of the needs of our churches today.

HARRY PILAND
Director, The Sunday School Department
The Sunday School Board of the Southern Baptist Convention

Contents

How to Get the Most Out of This Book

Let the creative juices of your mind flow to produce a greater church for the glory of God. At the end of each chapter or lengthy concept is a space for "Notes and Thoughts." Here you can write your own thoughts, ideas, and goals stimulated in your mind from my comments. You will discover that as you read this book, especially the second and third times, your ideas multiply. The results will be that you will find yourself writing many of your own creative ideas!

I will show you formulas, methods, and concepts that will lead you to succeed. These will stimulate your mind and bring out tremendous thoughts and ideas that are, and always have been, in your mind. Those thoughts and ideas, along with a little direction and guidance, will help you form a plan to reach your goal and bring visible and spiritual rewards you once thought came only to other church leaders.

1

Building and Changing a Mind-Set

Think Where to Start

The purpose of this book is to give ideas to church leaders to increase their congregation in all areas of church life.

Applying these concepts will affect the increase of:

- Church membership
- Sunday School enrollment
- Sunday School attendance
- Church Training attendance
- Baptisms
- Offerings
- Building
- Training leadership
- Mission gifts
- Music
- Mission organizations
- Other activities of the church

These concepts have been tried personally and proven by more than thirty years of experience in small churches of less than fifty members and large downtown churches of more than five thousand. These concepts are from experiences in associations, state conventions, and Convention-wide programs over the last fifteen years.

Some of the ideas the reader may not like. That is acceptable, for the author does not expect one to accept 100 percent of his concepts. He anticipates only an open mind. He hopes the reader will treat the material like a shopper walking through a supermarket. A shopper is not expected to buy the whole store, but gets a basket and selects those items she and her family have a taste for and can afford.

The author, for instance, does not like liver. He never buys liver from the meat section of the supermarket. It does not matter how you "bread it," "shred it," "boil it," "broil it," "slice it," or "dice it," he has a nerve in his throat that, the minute liver touches it, shouts out "LIVER!" And he gives it right back to you. He cannot swallow liver. He realizes, though, that some people like liver. He doesn't start a movement to ban liver from the market just because he doesn't like it. He just passes it by without a thought and leaves the liver for those buyers who have a taste for it.

Therefore, as you read, if you come to a concept or an idea that you cannot "swallow," pass it by—but don't stop reading. Just write the word *liver* in the margin and keep on reading. There will be some fried chicken, pork chops, ham, and other things you do like. There will be enough other ideas to fill your basket "abundantly above all that we ask or think" (Eph. 3:20) to help you accomplish those goals that you desire for your church.

Getting a Mind-Set for Growth

"As he thinketh in his heart, so is he" (Prov. 23:7). Motivation experts tell us that we become what we think about. What do you think about most of the time? Think success and you become successful. Think defeat, and you will be defeated. "To him that knoweth to do good, and doeth it not, to him it is sin" (Jas. 4:17). Therefore think positively, and solutions to problems will appear.

Concept 1: Activity in the Lord's work is a growth process. Many people, after they are converted, do not do much in the Lord's work because they do not know what to do. As leaders, this is where our ministry begins. In developing the Christian, we, like Paul, must realize that young Christians are "babes" in Christ and must begin on the "milk of the word" (1 Pet. 2:2).

Remember, Paul took three years in preparation after he was converted before he began preaching. And yet Paul (Saul) had been trained by Gamaliel in the old Hebrew law. He did not immediately begin preaching Christ Jesus.

Remember Moses? It required forty years in the wilderness to prepare him for God's purpose.

There are other examples in the Bible of people taking a period of time to grow into development for God's full purpose for their lives. Therefore, we should consider the growth process of people who accept and come to the Lord.

No one is fully grown at birth. There are three stages in life before a person becomes an adult. There is infancy, childhood, youth, then adulthood. Retarded physical growth can be harmful. Too rapid growth can present problems. Normal growth is most desirable.

The Bible is full of examples of comparison of the physical life to the spiritual life. "Grow in grace, and in the knowledge of our Lord and Saviour Jesus Christ" (2 Pet. 3:18).

With this in mind, we as leaders should realize and provide spiritual growth activities, concepts, and techniques for the people of all ages we lead in order to fulfill the above Scripture.

God has given us the ability to change. "Set your affection on things above" (Col. 3:2).

If we want to grow a church, we need to *think* growth constantly. We must *talk* growth continually. "But those things which proceed out of the mouth come forth from the heart" (Matt. 15:18).

We must *do* growth actions. "By their fruits ye shall know them" (Matt. 7:20).

We must *lead* our people to think, talk, and have growth actions. "Ye have not, because ye ask not" (Jas. 4:2*b*). Most people will do what you ask them to do. The problem is, we do not ask them. Most people will follow when you show them the way by your actions. You cannot lead others where you have not been unless you are willing to go also.

Growth Mind-Set Starts at the Pulpit

Many pastors do not realize the most *powerful place* of *promotion* is the *pulpit.* They do not realize the most *powerful person* of *promotion* is the *pastor.* Another realization often overlooked is that the *strongest* organization for carrying out the Great Commission is the *Sunday School.*

The worship hour is where the largest group of people hear one voice speaking of anything that happens all week long. Most people believe what they hear. A person develops feelings and convictions from what he hears, sees, and experiences. This being true, the pastor's voice from the pulpit has the greatest influence on the greatest number of people in what they do and believe.

Most people believe every word the preacher speaks from the pulpit. This is because he is the "called out one," the "man of the cloth," "God's chosen servant." There is a tremendous reverence for the pastor and a general acceptance of whatever he says. Therefore, we need to be keenly aware of what we say from the "sacred desk." We also need to be keenly *aware of what we do not say.* People not only believe what we say, they also believe what we do not say. Consequently, if *nothing* is said in the worship hour about the Sunday School, the Bible teaching hour, often people will develop an attitude that Sunday School must not be important and there may not be a need to attend it. The preacher never talks about it, so it must not be important, because the preacher only talks about important things. How subtly we destroy our own programs, and don't even realize we are doing it.

Many churches have gone a step further by eliminating the Sunday School and Church Training enrollment and attendance boards from the front of the auditorium. The reason given is that it takes away from the aesthetic value of the sanctuary. Dear friend, a part of the aesthetic value of a worship service is rejoicing over the number of people *enrolled* and *attending* the Bible study hour in study of God's Word. "Study to shew thyself approved" (2 Tim. 2:15). This is a part of "grow[ing] in grace and in the knowledge of our Lord" (2 Pet. 3:18).

I believe that the worship hour should be an extension and/or a continuation of the Bible teaching hour. However, most of the time it would be difficult to recognize that the Sunday School and worship hour are related. Sad, but true.

Negative teaching is being done by lack of visibility or verbalization of what happened the previous hour in Bible study.

Many churches have ceased making a Sunday School attendance report during the worship hour. A number of excuses are given as to why this is not done, but none are genuinely valid. By the way, do you know what an excuse is? It is a "skin of a reason stuffed with a lie."

In the worship service four things ought to be said about the Sunday School Bible teaching hour:

1. The Sunday School enrollment
2. The Sunday School attendance
3. The number of visits and/or contacts made last week

4. The number of new members that Sunday.

When giving recognition to the number of new members, do not say, "We had three new members," but rather call the person by name who did the enrolling. For example: "John Smith's class had a new member. Martha White's class had a new member, and Jane Jones' third grade had a new member." And perhaps you might want to give the names of the new members. Give recognition to those people who are doing the job. Recognition motivates and will motivate others to enroll people. It highlights the importance of enrollment by calling names. If your church is of such size that the number of names would be long, say ten or more, list the names in the following week's order of service and call attention to the names listed. Recognition is necessary. "Well done, thou good and faithful servant" (Matt. 25:21).

It is hard to realize that the majority of churches more than ten years old have less than 50 percent of their resident membership enrolled in Sunday School. Dear pastor, this should tell us something concerning the importance of the relationship between the worship hour and the Sunday School. We have a tremendous obligation within our own four walls. Many of the people in the worship hour are not enrolled in Bible study. They need to be enrolled and attending. Every church member needs to be enrolled in Sunday School Bible teaching. You, pastor, could lead many to enroll by saying, "Some of you people in this worship hour are not enrolled in Bible study. You need Bible study if you are going to grow as a Christian. Therefore, reach in the pew pocket, take out the enrollment card, fill it out and drop it in the offering plate. We want all of our church members enrolled in Bible study." Many pastors who have started this have told me, "Neil, we are enrolling two or three every Sunday during the worship hour. Thanks for the idea."

There is a reason we talk about contacts. This declares to

the whole congregation that visitation is important. We believe in reaching absentees and prospects.

The following pages will give a variety of methods and concepts to motivate different personalities in a broader scope of the enrolling-attendance-visitation contact and the reaching-people ministry.

In leading people to grow both spiritually and numerically, do not expect rapid growth overnight, for that would be abnormal.

Pray for and lead people into a normal spiritual growth pattern. A caution to keep in mind is the creation of a "be-like-me" syndrome. When God made us, he made each of us unique individuals with a wide variety of personalities. No two people are exactly alike; therefore, we as leaders should use multiple variations and ways to accomplish the task God has set before us.

When we use various methods with different personalities a broader scope of people can and will be reached and used. "I am made all things to all men, that I might by all means save some" (1 Cor. 9:22). Therefore, with the above in mind, use the pulpit to reach people for Sunday School Bible study.

Compelling People to Come

I grew up on a small farm in northern Indiana, and we lived near a Christian conference ground. My mother wanted her four sons to be exposed to as many Christian concepts as possible. Therefore, through the summer months when many religious conference leaders were preaching, she would say, "Boys, how would you like to go to the conference grounds and go swimming today?" Of course, four cheers would go up immediately. She would say, "All right, let's get our chores done, and we will walk the two miles to the conference grounds and go swimming."

Needless to say, it did not take us long to hoe the garden,

clean the barn, feed the chickens, ducks, goats, and get all the necessary household chores done in about an hour and a half. My mother had a compelling spirit for her sons to hear the Word and good preaching.

She also had a desire for us to learn the Word and had unique ways of teaching us the Scriptures. As we walked to the conference grounds, she would take one Scripture verse for us to memorize on the way over, and another Scripture verse to memorize on the way back.

I have learned more Scripture in the rhythm or the cadence of a march than I have standing or sitting still. I think somewhere she picked up the concept of "As you are going do these things." With each step we would say a Scripture in rhythm. So we boys literally had the Scripture marched into our brains and bodies. It took me till age twenty-five to break myself of the habit of quoting Scripture in cadence.

Another unique method my mother had was to tape Scripture verses in various places in the house. We learned the Scripture by awareness. For instance, "Taste and see that the Lord is good" (Ps. 34:8) was taped on the refrigerator door. Over the kitchen sink was the verse, "Whosoever drinketh of this water shall thirst again: but whosoever drinketh of the water that I shall give him shall never thirst" (John 4:13,14).

The Scripture verses would change from time to time. For instance, "And I will wipe Jerusalem as a man wipeth a dish, wiping it, and turning it upside down" appeared. Then Mom would say, "You see, boys, the Lord intended for men to wash dishes." I especially liked the one on the refrigerator door that said, "He that putteth his trust in the Lord shall be made fat" (Prov. 28:25). You see, my Mom is a little overweight and had to justify it. The verse on the back door was, "Behold, I stand at the door, and knock: if any man hear my voice, and open the door, I will come in" (Rev. 3:20). As you walked up the stairs to the bedroom, on each step was a word of a verse, "The steps of a good man are ordered by the Lord"

(Ps. 37:23). On the headboard of the bed was "Come ye . . . apart . . . and rest awhile" (Mark 6:31). Then when you lay your head on the pillow and looked up at the ceiling you would see, "Rest in the Lord" (Ps. 37:7). Mom has a real sense of humor. She could have made money by giving the Coca Cola people methods of awareness promotion.

All of this was not bad. At the time I thought it was kind of difficult, and that she was pressing a little hard. When I went to the seminary twenty years later, in Dr. C. E. Autry's evangelism class we were required to memorize 100 Scripture verses. To my amazement, I had already learned most of them as a child. "Train up a child in the way he should go: and when he is old, he will not depart from it" (Prov. 22:6).

Needless to say, I have a deep respect for parents who have a compelling spirit to teach and train their children in the ways of the Lord.

I remember hearing a preacher tell many stories and testimonies at the conference grounds. One was about the conversion experience of an alcoholic at the Pacific Garden Mission, downtown Chicago. God's Holy Spirit had gotten hold of him one night as the preacher preached, and he accepted the Lord as Savior. Immediately full of God's Spirit and desire to see one of his alcoholic friends come to know Christ, too, he went out on the streets and found his friend in a tavern nearby. He told the friend of his personal experience with the Lord, and about his having been saved, and said he wanted the friend to get saved, also. The friend said, "I don't believe I want to do that." The new convert answered, "But you've got to! I heard that preacher say that I am to 'Go out into the highways and hedges, and compel them to come in' (Luke 14:23), and I want you to come and hear this man preach the gospel."

The alcoholic buddy said, "I'm not going to do that."

The new convert replied, "Yes, you are," and a little argument started back and forth.

"No, I'm not!"

"Yes, you are!"

"No, I'm not!"

Then the new convert, knowing only one meaning for the word *compel,* just drew back his arm and popped his alcoholic friend right on the jaw, knocking him to his knees. The new convert said, "I've got to *compel* you to come and hear the gospel. Now, come on!"

The friend staggered to his feet, saying, "I believe I'll go." He, too, was converted that night.

Now, I'm not suggesting that we go out and hit our friends in the face with our fists if they don't come to hear the message preached and possibly accept Christ. But I am saying that we should have the same inner drive that this new convert had, to the point that we will do whatever it takes to get a friend to hear the Word so the Holy Spirit can work in that life and he accepts Christ. Our problem today is we have lost our *compelling* desire to bring people to hear the gospel preached and taught. Pray for compulsion. God will give it to you. We have become Christians of convenience rather than conviction. "How shall they believe in him of whom they have not heard?" (Rom. 10:14).

I Might Offend

It is my belief that in the last twenty years, Christians have become very passive in reaching people. Many times we hear people say, "I'm afraid I will offend those people and they may not come to hear the gospel of Christ." Dear friend, that is a feeble excuse. The greatest offense that is taking place is allowing that person to go to hell and not saying a word about it.

We need to be more aggressive in reaching people. We need to be more forward. We need to be more outspoken.

Christ was loving and caring, but aggressive. Very few incidents in the life of Christ are mentioned in all four Gospels. For all four Gospel writers to describe a certain act emphasizes its importance. The act of Jesus' casting out the money changers from the Temple with a whip is found in all four Gospels— Matthew 21, Mark 11, Luke 19, and John 2. Jesus also was aggressive when he rebuked Peter, Mary, Martha, and the sea. Other incidents are also mentioned in the Gospels.

We have preached and taught too much the gentle side of Christ, which is all true. But we have not presented much of the aggressive side of Christ. There needs to be both the loving/caring and the aggressive sides of Christ. Work toward a balance.

Losing the Call

One of the greatest problems today in our churches is that people, preachers, and paid staff are not genuinely concentrating on and thinking about reaching people. This is evident when you study the major denominational growth record for the past one hundred years. You will discover a sharp tapering off by all major denominations in the past twenty to twenty-five years.

At the first half of this century, there was strong encouragement in the reaching aspect of the ministry, to the place that Baptists, for example, got out on the streets, knocked on doors inviting, yes, even compelling in many instances, people to come and be enrolled in Sunday School. Then in the fifties and sixties, an attitude of sophistication seemed to take hold of the churches in most denominations. It was felt that it was no longer necessary to knock on doors, but to provide quality teaching and facilities. Reaching was downplayed. If quality teaching and facilities were provided, it was felt people would flock to the churches. Time has proved this to be untrue. After a quarter of a century of this attitude and philosophy, all major denominations have lost membership. It takes more than quality teaching and beautiful facilities. It takes aggressive outreach and door knocking. There is a real need for an emphasis on reaching once again. You cannot separate the two. You need quality and quantity.

The real need and emphasis now is toward quantity. Therefore, the following pages will emphasize strongly the reaching aspect. It is my belief that reaching needs to have priority, as there can be no teaching if the people are not there to be taught. Therefore, underline in your own mind the real need for reaching. If necessary, begin your mind-set change now.

A car dealer friend of mine in Arkansas had a sign in his office that said, "When you have stopped changing, you have stopped." I hope I never stop changing for something better. Principles never change. Methods always do.

Oldsmobile Concept

My youngest brother's father-in-law owned an Oldsmobile dealership in the city of Chicago. He had a practice every Monday morning of gathering all employees in the shop area at 7 AM. More than sixty employees worked for him. They would form a big semicircle. As part of the emphasis of the week's work he would walk around the circle and ask each person two questions. The first question was, "Who do you know who needs a car?" The second question was, "How can we sell more Oldsmobiles?" Each person had to come up with two answers, regardless of how ridiculous the answer may have sounded. What was he doing? He was establishing a mind-set for sales for the week. He asked these questions of all the employees. Here was a man who serviced automobiles. Here was a mechanic. Another person was in bookkeeping; another in sales. Another washed cars. Another did brake repairs. Each person had a specialty. Each person had to answer the two questions, "Who do you know who needs a car?" "How can we sell more Oldsmobiles?"

If employees did not show up at 7 AM or come up with answers, it was not long until they no longer were employed. That's called motivation. You see, the owner of the company had ONE desire—to sell Oldsmobiles. He was aware of a sociological principle; that is, every person influences ten other people in one way or another. This is known as the basic circle of influence. He had more than sixty employees who worked for him, so he knew immediately he could move into a minimum of six hundred homes of potential customers for Oldsmobiles. He was teaching all personnel to be sensitive to sales and look for potential customers. Let me illustrate.

Let's assume one of the mechanics is bowling on Friday night. As he and his friends are sitting together waiting their turns to bowl, one of the bowlers says to the mechanic, "You know, I nearly didn't make it tonight."

"Oh, how come?"

"Well, my old car just chugged getting here and nearly quit running, and I had a terrible time getting here tonight."

Don't you know that in that mechanic's brain a bell just went off—DING, DING, DING, DING—and he immediately said, "Listen, I can get you a good deal at Blue Island Oldsmobile. In fact, we can give you more for your old car than you can get anywhere else. Let me call John, our salesman, right now, and he can talk to you over the phone, line you up, tell you what he can give you for your car, and what might be available. In fact, he can bring the car by the bowling alley and you can drive it home tonight." The man is more apt to buy the Oldsmobile because of the confidence and assurance the mechanic gave.

There's another aspect to this concept. Because the friend did get a good deal and was very happy about it, when one of his friends says to him, "I'm thinking about buying a car," that same bell will ring in the new owner's mind. Then he'll say, "Listen, I got an excellent deal over at Blue Island Oldsmobile. I got a good deal from John, the salesman. Let me call him and you can get a good deal, too."

When you follow this principle even to the second generation of contacts in their circles of influence, you have now moved into six thousand homes as potential customers for automobiles.

I can hear some of you thinking, *Well, now, what has this Oldsmobile story got to do with church work and reaching people? This author should be concerned with reaching people and saving souls, not selling Oldsmobiles.* Dear friend, I have just given you the greatest concept and method for reaching people. It's a mind-set I'm working on. You see, the Oldsmobile dealer established a mind-set for all of his employees on Monday morning to think sales all week long and how they could sell more cars. He also was using another principle. In a sense, he put all the employees on an equal level, with a common goal—whether they were vice-presidents of the company or persons who greased automobiles. The owner believes that God gave every person a brain to think with, and that a person who greases cars may come up with an idea to sell Oldsmobiles. The vice-president or salesmen of the company are not the only ones with brains to think sales.

Now, how does this apply to us in the church—preacher, Sunday School director, teacher, worker, each one who leads a group of people? Whether you're teaching a class, or you are a department leader or a Sunday School director, you have an influence over a group of people. You can lead people to think growth.

Preacher, what would happen if some Sunday night you preached a sermon on reaching people. Then you took several minutes to go down the row of the congregation and ask each person two questions: "Who do you know who is not attending or enrolled in Sunday Bible study?" "How can we reach more people for Christ?" It is possible you will pick up more prospects than you ever dreamed of. You will begin to develop a mind-set for growth.

Here is an idea you may want to consider. In a morning service hand a three-by-five card to everyone. Ask the people to write the name of someone they know who is not attending a Bible study on Sunday. Next, ask for that person's phone number. If the phone number is unknown ask the people to write the name of the street the person lives on. Tell them a church worker will look up the phone number and address. Ask the members to write and circle their own names at the bottom of the card and place in the offering plate. Using this process, you have just received information for an instant prospect.

Later in the book, I will show you other ways to find prospects and how to enroll people by telephone. This is another way you have begun a mind-set for growth with adults, youth, and yes, even with children.

Once a quarter or twice a year, use the three-by-five card concept in the congregation departments, or classes, encouraging people to give names. This concept will be explained more in detail in the next chapter under "Instant Prospects." Begin now to establish a mind-set for growth. At workers' meetings, what would happen if you asked the two questions: "Who do you know who's not attending a Bible study?" "How can we reach more people for Christ?" This will generate enthusiasm, encourage a mind-set for reaching people, and will produce prospects and ways to reach people.

Some of you are saying, "Everybody won't respond." Well, that's all right. Take those who will respond. Think positively. Think possibilities. If you pick up eight, ten, or twelve prospects every Wednesday night or Sunday, names of those people who are not enrolled in Bible study, by the end of the year you could have more than five hundred prospects who could and will be reached. Those prospects have a close identification with someone already involved in your church work.

Sunday School teachers in classes on Sunday morning, what would happen if the teachers asked members in their classes, "Who do you know who's not enrolled in Bible study?" "How can we reach more people for Christ?" The prospect is going to be a neighbor, a person a member works with, a friend, someone a member goes to school with, or a relative. By experience, I have discovered that most prospects are going to be of the same sex and approximately the same age as the person who lists them.

Begin asking members for prospects. Begin the mind-set for growth. If you talk growth, think growth, act growth, you will have growth.

Later in the book, I list twenty-four other ways to find prospects and reach people for Sunday School enrollment.

Never Commit

"I don't believe in making a commitment to attend, give, or teach," is a statement often heard in church work. Yet that same person thinks of himself as a good Christian. It would be interesting to hear the answers of the person who says, "I do not believe in making a commitment."

The following questions could be asked of that person.

1. Do you tell a doctor when he prescribes medicine that you will take it only if you feel like it?
2. Do you feel no responsibility toward feeding, clothing, and educating your children?
3. Do you tell your boss you don't have to follow his instructions?

4. Do you go to work whenever you want to?
5. Do you pay your bills?
6. Do you run around on your wife?

If a person does not believe in making a commitment, how does he face the questions above?

The Scripture says, "Commit thy way unto the Lord; trust also in him; and he shall bring it to pass" (Ps. 37:5). No commitment, no salvation.

Notes and Thoughts

2

Speaking from the Pulpit

Instant Prospects

If a church is going to grow it needs prospects and an up-to-date prospect file.

Do you know how many people should be in a prospect file? Some well-meaning person might say, "The whole city." Well, that may not be true. Some might say, "A thousand people." Well, that might not be true either. There is a logical answer. The *minimum* number of prospects in a prospect file should equal the Sunday School enrollment. Therefore if you have one hundred people enrolled in Sunday School, you should have *at least* one hundred prospects in file for the Sunday School.

Some church leaders will say, "We know all the people in this town, and there are just no prospects." How many times I have heard this, especially during a "reaching people" emphasis, such as ACTION enlargement or growth campaigns.

Here is a way you can have instant prospects next Sunday and never leave the auditorium. I briefly referred to this idea in the preceding chapter. Place three-by-five cards in the backs of the pews or insert them in the bulletin. When you use this process, let me encourage you to proceed slowly through the process so people will be able to keep up with what you want done. In fact, it would be good for you to take a card and write the things you are asking the people to do. This will help you to keep pace with them, and not run ahead of them. I use a large chalkboard on the platform so all can not only hear what I am saying but see as I write. This helps them to think about what I am saying. Ask everyone to take a card. Encourage children and youth also to take a card. It is sad when most of the things we speak about from the pulpit are spoken to adults. We rarely speak to children and youth. We talk about winning people to the Lord and reaching people for Christ, but the whole concept in the minds of most leaders is to enlist the adults. Occasionally we think and direct the conversation to older youth during Youth Week. But we do not think about children beginning to think or act on reaching people. The Scripture tells us "Train up a child in the way he should go: and when he is old, he will not depart from it" (Prov. 22:6).

Therefore, if that Scripture is true, we should begin to teach children to reach people for Christ by inviting their friends to Sunday School and to teach them soul-winning verses. Children have friends they play with, schoolmates, relatives, and other people they come into contact with. We should begin teaching them at least an awareness of the spiritual responsibilities of a Christian.

Now back to the instant prospect concept. Ask everyone in the congregation to take a three-by-five card. Ask everyone in the congregation to hold the card in the air. The purpose is to make sure everyone has a card. If you see someone who does not have a card, ask an usher to give that person a card.

The next step is for everyone to think of reaching people. You might say, "We need to have a mind-set for reaching people. We need to have a mind-set to think about reaching people. Therefore, I want you to think of one person— someone you know who is not attending Bible study on Sunday morning."

Leader, numbers will work for you if you work them. They will work against you if you don't work them correctly, so lead people to think of one person only, someone who is not attending Bible study anywhere on Sunday morning.

Leader, you can help the members of the congregation think of people they know. You may ask them, "What about the persons you *work* with? Does one of them need to be enrolled in Sunday School? Boys and girls, young people, it may be a person you are in *school* with. What about a *neighbor* of yours? Is that neighbor attending Sunday School? What about some of your good *friends?* Are they attending Sunday School? What about relatives? Are they attending Sunday School? Think about someone you know who is not attending Sunday School." You see, the name they write probably is going to be a member of one of the five groups mentioned—a neighbor, a friend, a coworker, a schoolmate, or a relative. There is a sixth possibility, and that is the person himself who is in the congregation, so you could say, "If you *yourself* are here today and not enrolled in Bible study, put your name on the card." I use the chalkboard and write the six possibilities, one word for each possibility mentioned. This process helps their thinking.

An interesting thing I have discovered in this process is that the majority of the time the name given is that of a person of the approximate age of the person who gives the name, and usually of the same sex. Another discovery is that the individual will give you the best prospect known. You see, in this process the person giving the information sifts through his mind the names of the people he knows—relatives, friends, persons he works with, schoolmates, or neighbors, thinking about each one. He thinks to himself: "Who do I know? My relatives? No, they are not prospects. My friend? No, he's not one. The person I work with? Yes, he is a good prospect. I'll write that person's name." He has mentally sifted through his acquaintances and given one name, and it generally is the best prospect he can think of. So the most potential "hot" prospect is given. There will be some duplication. There will be some names given of people already enrolled. This will generally be less than ten percent. So expect it but don't let it bother you. After all, whatever number you received is more than what you had, and it is *fresh* information for your prospect file.

The next step is to write underneath the name they have given the phone number of the person. Most of the time, people will know the phone number. However, say to the congregation, "If you do not know the phone number write the name of the street the person lives on. Someone in the church office will look up the phone number."

Next step: At the bottom of the card, ask the person to sign his name and put a circle around it. This allows those working with the cards to know who gave the information in the event there is additional information needed. Contact can be made for further information if needed. It will also be used when contacting the prospect for enrollment. If the writer of the card prefers his name not be used, he can so indicate on the card or leave his name off the card.

This process gives you a list of instant prospects who have at least an indirect relationship to the church already. They will be your "hottest" prospects.

The first time I used this idea was in Independence, Missouri. I was preaching to a congregation of about 350. We received 127 cards. The ten duplications were removed. Most of the duplications came from the children, for some listed the same friend. I have discovered you will get about 25 to 30 percent of a congregation to respond to this process.

That afternoon 68 of the 117 were contacted by phone. You will find approximately 50 percent of the people home on Sunday afternoon. Of the 68 contacted, 28 were enrolled. The following Sunday, 20 of them attended. Here is the conversation that was used on the telephone to enroll them.

"This is Neil Jackson from the First Baptist Church. Your

good friend Frank Smith gave us your name and said you are not enrolled in Sunday School on Sunday morning. Could we enroll you with your good friend, Frank Smith, in our Sunday School?"

Four things could take place in the mind of the person being called.

First, this type of contact legitimizes the caller. The person on the other end of the line might say to himself, "This is not some religious 'nut,' because my good friend Frank Smith would not give my name to a religious 'nut.' "

Second, it legitimizes the church. Because the good friend Frank Smith would not give his name to some "weird" church.

Third, it says to the prospect that the good friend, Frank Smith, is interested in him spiritually.

Fourth, it can say to adults, "I can sit in Sunday School with my good friend, Frank Smith. I have been reluctant to go to a strange Sunday School class where I don't know anyone. If I can sit with my good friend, I'll go. Yes, you can enroll me."

I can hear some organizational purists saying this destroys the organization by allowing a person to sit with his good friend. Let us not lose sight of our priority, which is to *reach people*. If I can get a person in the Sunday School to hear the gospel of Christ, I will set the grading system aside for a time to get that person. I am people-centered first, system-centered second. I will worry about my grading system when October comes. This is what Arthur Flake teaches. "Each year bring your system back into line." The grading system is an educational process. The new person has to first come in to hear, to learn, to experience, to grow. Given a period of time, he can learn the system. This is why we're interested in the person first and the grading system second.

Please do not misread me at this point. *You need the grading system.* It basically has three purposes or functions: one, to give responsibility to a class for a prospect of a certain age;

two, to give direction to the visitor when he comes as to whose class he should attend; three, to give balance to the classes. There are other reasons, but these three are primary. Therefore, be people-centered.

My experience has been in enrolling people in Sunday School over the telephone, you will average a success rate of about one out of every four phone calls.

Additional Ways to Find Prospects

Take an inside census and gather the names of unenrolled parents, brothers, and sisters of the children who are enrolled in Sunday School. This can add approximately 30 to 50 percent or more of the prospects of what your Sunday School enrollment is.

A third list of prospects is all church members not enrolled in Sunday School. The way to discover this is to take your entire church roll and place it alongside the Sunday School roll. If a church member's name is not listed on the Sunday School roll, put it on the list. This makes the third prospect list. Every church member can and should be enrolled somewhere in Sunday School.

There are nine areas where church members can be enrolled. They are as follows. *One,* of course, is the regular Sunday School. *Second* is a pastor's class. A pastor's class is designed for church members not enrolled in Sunday School and could last twenty-six weeks. When it terminates, move those people into the regular organization. Some pastors may choose to continue the pastor's class. However those class members who have the capabilities for working elsewhere in the Sunday School should be led into service. We are "saved to serve, not sit." A *third* area is the cradle roll. The *fourth* is the homebound ministry. The *fifth* is special education (for the retarded). The *sixth,* is a Wednesday night Sunday School for people who work on Sunday. The *seventh* is a language ministry, and *eighth* is the ministry to the deaf. The *ninth* is for those away at school. Now you see there is no excuse for anyone not being enrolled in the Sunday School. There can be a class or department for everyone.

Here are other ways to build up the prospect file:

1. Get the names of all visitors. Visit and add their names to the file.
2. Use the "New Name" source. Visit and add their names to the file.
3. Use a "referral system" regularly, by department or by the whole Sunday School.
4. Visit house-to-house. Use the program of "ACTION," "Open Enrollment," or "People Search."
5. Use the cross-reference telephone directory for a telephone survey.

When You Join the Church — You Join the Whole Church

James 4:2 says, "Ye have not, because ye ask not." We need to do some real thinking in the area of how negligent we are in asking people to be a part of our total church program. It becomes a challenge when one realizes that in most churches over ten years old, 30 to 50 percent of the resident members are not enrolled in Sunday School. My experience has been that approximately 60 to 90 percent of the Sunday School members are not enrolled in Training Union. Also you are doing well if 10 percent of the Sunday School members are enrolled in the mission organizations. You can see how little we are reaching our total congregation with all of the fundamental purposes of a church.

It would be good to emphasize the concept that "when you

join the church, you join the *whole* church"—that is, you automatically are enrolled in Sunday School, Church Training, and a mission organization.

When I was minister of education at First Baptist Church, New Orleans, Louisiana, this was the practice used. Dr. J. D. Grey was pastor at the time, and would give the invitation. I would receive people down front along with several of the deacons. We used the principal that when you joined the church you joined the whole church. When a man joined our church, we would say to him, "You have just joined First Baptist Church. You have joined the Sunday School, the Training Union and the Brotherhood." When a lady joined, we would say, "You have joined First Baptist Church. You have joined the Sunday School, the Training Union, and the Woman's Missionary Union (now Baptist Women). For when you join our church, these organizations are all a part of our church." During my three and one-half years with Dr. Grey, I had only one person to refuse. He said, "Let me tell you one thing. I've joined your church for one reason and one reason only, and that is business. I will attend one Sunday a month. I will send you a check one Sunday a month, but I'll not be a part of your Sunday School, Church Training, and for sure I'll not be a part of your Brotherhood. Do you understand?" If I had been sharp at the time I would have asked, "Which Sunday?" I turned to Dr. Grey and told him what the man said. I asked Dr. Grey what should we do. He said, "Take his money."

We need to understand a principle. Many people do not do, because we do not ask them to do. They do not join because we do not ask them to join. They do not become a part because we do not expect them to be a part. Therefore, ask and expect them to be a part.

I have not been a Southern Baptist all my life. As a mountain missionary living by faith in the mountains of Arkansas, I was winning people to the Lord, baptizing them in a creek, and forgetting about them. There was no concept of a total ministry and purpose of the church. But I saw Southern Baptists with a *plan,* a *program,* and a *direction* and said to myself, "This is the way to go." In the spring of 1953 my wife and I were baptized into the fellowship of First Baptist Church, Ozark, Arkansas. My greatest problem in coming into the denomination was being put under the water the third time. If it were baptism that got you into heaven, I'd know I'd made it! By the way, it took me six months to work through doctrinally the question on baptism—thanks to a patient pastor.

After I had joined the church and was baptized, about two weeks later, someone came to me and said, "Neil, you need to join the Sunday School."

I said, "I joined your church two weeks ago. Isn't the Sunday School a part of the church?"

"Oh, no, that's something different."

So I joined the Sunday School.

About four weeks later someone said, "Neil, you need to join the Training Union."

I said, "I joined the church six weeks ago. Isn't the Training Union a part of the church?"

"Oh, no, that's something different."

Then about six weeks after that, someone said, "Neil, you need to join the Brotherhood."

And I asked, "Isn't the Brotherhood a part of the church?"

"Oh, no, that's something different."

You see, as an outsider coming into a Baptist church, I had no knowledge that all of these organizations of the church had to be joined separately. I assumed that when you join the church you joined the *whole* church. And all of these organizations were a part of the church.

Here is my point. Many people are not a part of these organizations because they have never been asked or expected to be a part. Consequently, they are lost to those areas that develop the Christian in spiritual growth. I was a person who wanted to be a part of the whole organization, and I was eager to be a part. There was a loss of twelve weeks' time that could have been benefiting me had the attitude been that when you join the church, you join the *whole* church. What might have happened if no one had asked me to join those programs of the church? It leaves a large area for a majority of people to be lost from the total spiritual program of the church. In one sense, this was not a great deal different from what I had been doing in the mountains: winning, baptizing, and forgetting. They need to be enlisted in all the programs to "grow in grace, and in the knowledge of our Lord and Saviour Jesus Christ" (2 Pet. 3:18).

Therefore, let me encourage you to lead people toward the concept that when you join the church, you join the entire church and all of its programs.

If some programs are not important, let's drop them.

By experience I have learned people will protect themselves and indicate either verbally or by nonattendance their desire not to become involved. Keep in mind that our responsibility as ministers, workers, and teachers, is to reach people and to develop them in the greatest way we possibly can.

People will only do what they want to do, what they're asked to do, and what we might expect them to do. "Ye have not, because ye ask not" (Jas. 4:2*b*). You also have not because you expect not. Therefore, let's expect to be a part of the total program. When you join the church, you join the whole church.

Notes and Thoughts

Preacher Points the Way

Another mind-set for growth is identifying a new church member with a Sunday School class quickly. The preacher will need to know his Sunday School organization. This will not be too difficult, especially in a small church. In a large church this information can be indicated on the back of the new member card being filled out by the person receiving the information at the altar.

When a person joins the church, the pastor can say, "John, come down front. This fellow has joined our church today. He's a member for your department. He's a member for your class. Stand alongside him." John comes down and stands alongside the new member, gives him a handshake, welcomes him, and makes him feel wanted. Then after everyone has walked past and given him the right hand of Christian fellowship, making him feel welcome, John says, "Come with me. I'll take you to our classroom. You will be able to see the classroom and know where it meets. This way, next Sunday you can find it when you come." John takes the new member upstairs and says, "You notice our room is 202. We meet at 9:30." John then goes back downstairs past the church office, picks up a quarterly, and says, "This is your quarterly. I'm your teacher." He writes his name, John Smith, across the top of the quarterly, puts the room number, 202, and the time, 9:30. John then says, "We are expecting you. Do you need a ride?" He gives the quarterly to the new member.

Do you realize what happened in just a few minutes? There were five things that took place: (1) teacher identification; (2) classroom location; (3) literature distribution; (4) time of meeting; and (5) a spirit of expectation. The next Sunday, when the new member walks through the door, people don't look at him like a total stranger with blank looks on their faces. Instead, the teacher, with excitement, says, "Here is our new member, Frank Jones. He joined our church last Sunday. We're delighted to have you. Welcome. Come on in."

Another mind-set is established. The piece of literature becomes a motivational tool for expectation all week long. It is silently saying to the new member, "Come to Sunday School; come to Sunday School; they expect you; they expect you." He may forget the location. He may forget the time. He may forget the teacher's name, but he picks up the quarterly and it says, "John Smith, teacher, Room 202, 9:30 AM." "He's looking for me. He knows me, he expects me. I've got to attend."

That is a motivational mind-set for growth. So, dear pastor, when people join your church, lead them to join your whole church. Develop the leadership to identify quickly with the new church member. I hope these are some ideas that you can use and begin to develop a mind-set for growth, beginning with yourself. If you don't have it, no one else is going to catch it. If you want growth, *think* growth. If you want growth, *talk* growth. If you want growth, *act* growth. If you want growth, *expect* growth. James 4:2b says, "Ye have not, because ye ask not." Take these motivational growth ideas and use them.

Notes and Thoughts

Enroll the Worship Hour Visitors

Do you want to enroll additional members in Sunday School? Do you want to overcome the barrier that some Sunday School leaders put up of not enrolling anyone in Sunday School unless he attends three straight Sundays? If you do, I suggest you take this action. During the worship hour, when you recognize the visitors, say, "Welcome. We're delighted to have you. We want you to be a part of our Sunday School Bible teaching hour. As you fill out the visitor card, across the top of the card write, 'Enroll me,' and we will enroll you in a class today. Someone from that class will visit you this week and bring you a quarterly."

Or you may possibly indicate that there are Sunday School enrollment cards in the back of the pew. Ask the visitor to fill out an enrollment card and place it in the offering plate. Many churches will pick up new enrollees every Sunday using these methods. It will begin a mind-set for growth with people in the congregation to constantly be aware of enrolling new people as the leader from the pulpit is doing.

People will believe and follow what you say, pastor. It will overcome the resistance of expecting people to attend three Sundays before they are asked to enroll in a class. Incidentally, did it ever occur to you that the practice of three Sundays before we ask people to enroll has a similarity to an Old Testament attitude? Do you remember the passage telling of the people who were in captivity wandering and they cried unto the Lord, "Lord, how can we sing the songs of Zion out here in the wilderness. We have to be back in Jerusalem to be able to worship." The attitude is very similar when teachers say, "Preacher, how can you enroll in the main auditorium or outside the church when the people have to be back in the classroom? They have to be in the classroom before they can be enrolled." Do you see the similarity? Remember, enroll people anytime, anywhere, under any circumstances, as long as they agree. The worship hour is an ideal place to enroll people in Sunday School.

The surprising thing is you can enroll some of your church members who presently are not enrolled in Sunday School yet have been church members for a number of years.

The following approach may *not* be your style or your way of doing things, but catch the concept and adapt it to your personality and style. While preaching in a church of about six hundred, I had the following experience. During the worship hour, preaching on the need for being enrolled in Sunday School, I turned to the organist and said, "Are you enrolled in Sunday School?" She said, "No." I asked, "How long have you been organist?" She answered, "Three years."

I then asked, "Why aren't you enrolled in Sunday School?"

Her answer was, "No one ever asked me. I was a night club entertainer when I was saved. The church needed an organist, but never asked me to be a member of a Sunday School class."

I then enrolled her right then and there during the worship hour.

Still being led by the Spirit of God, I turned to a lady in the third row and asked, "Lady, are you enrolled in Sunday School?"

She said, "No."

I said, "How long have you been coming?"

Her answer, "Five weeks."

I said, "Why aren't you enrolled in Sunday School?"

She said, "No one has ever asked me or my daughter."

I said, "Ushers, bring enrollment cards and let's enroll these two people."

I turned to the choir and asked how many were not enrolled in Sunday School. Two more were enrolled from the choir. I asked who else in the congregation was not enrolled. Twelve people were enrolled in Sunday School that day in the auditorium. It comes back to the basic statement of James 4:2b, "Ye have not, because ye ask not."

People are wanting to be enrolled, but we as leaders fail to give them the opportunities. We assume that when new persons walk through the door, *they* are supposed to be aggressive. They are to find their way to a Sunday School class. They are to ask to be enrolled. This is a fallacy. They are not going to do it. We, the leaders and workers, need to have an aggressive growth concept. We need to reach out to enroll and give direction to the people. Therefore, ask!

A Gallup poll taken in the spring of 1980 of people who do not belong to anyone's church asked: "Would you join a church?" More than 50 percent indicated they would. Then when asked why they had not joined a church, the response was, "No one has asked us."

In January 1979, a new mission in Goose Creek, South Carolina, set goals using the Growth Spiral concept. They set as their goal to have 150 enrolled by January, 1980, one year later. In November 1979, they had reached an enrollment of 126. The Sunday morning I was there, there were 86 in the worship service. Enrollment cards were passed out to the congregation. Each person was asked to fill out an enrollment card to "update" the information in the church office. Some of the records the church office had were not complete, such as addresses, phone numbers, birth dates, full names, and so forth. When we went through the cards after the service, it was discovered we had enrolled 12 additional people in Sunday School during the morning worship hour. Some people "thought" they were on a Sunday School roll but were not. Every church should have a central Sunday School record file.

It may be good periodically to consider using the same method during the worship hour of having everyone present fill out an enrollment card for Sunday School to "update" the information. You also will discover you have added additional new members to the Sunday School. Even though many people have been attending, they have not been asked to join, or may think they are on the Sunday School rolls when they are not.

Incidentally, the mission reached its goal. It is running more than one hundred in attendance in just one year, from twenty-five enrolled in its beginning.

So you see, you can grow if you have a mind-set to grow and are willing to try new ways. It reminds me again of the sign I saw inside the car dealer's office, "When you have stopped changing, you have stopped." One of the problems we are facing today is an unwillingness to change our old methods and old ways. Consequently, we have stopped growing.

Don't read me wrong. Principles never change, but concepts and methods constantly change. Therefore, if you want to grow, be willing to change.

Notes and Thoughts

3

Broadening the Mind-Set Base for Visitation

Visitation – The Ministry

Visitation is necessary for a church to live.
Visitation prevents stagnation because of new people.
Visitation revitalizes the person who becomes involved.
Visitation creates insights into community needs.
Visitation develops growth, both numerical and spiritual.

The General Concept of Visitation

When one speaks of visitation, the meaning or semantics of the word says only one type of contacting people. If I were to write the word *Visitation* on the chalkboard, and ask, "What goes through your mind when you see the word *Visitation?*" you might suggest the words, "prospect," "new members," "soul-winners," "Thursday, 7:00-9:00 PM," "dedication," "concern," "absentee," "fear," "darkness," "dogs," etc. There are a number of words that go through people's minds when they see the word *visitation*. But because of the meaning of the word, there is one type of visitation that is strongly identified. It means to them physically, on a certain day of the week, getting up out of the chair, out of the house, and going some place to knock on someone's door. It's a door-knocking type concept of visitation.

In order to change the mind-set of one type, one day only

syndrome, ask for the names of people who can and will visit or make contacts on other days of the week. Put the *emphasis* on contacts on any day. "Give us your name if you made contacts last week." This *does not do away* with a special day set aside for visitation. That is necessary.

Let us begin to broaden our mind-set of outreach, broadening our whole concept of thinking in this area. Let us use the word *contact*. The moment we move the mind-set to the word *contact*, we open the door beyond the door-knocking concept, and open the opportunity to a broader scope of reaching people. We open the fuller use of the telephone, postcards, and of a new concept called C. C. C.

Contacts Using the C. C. C. Method

C. C. C. stands for Constant Contact Consciousness. This method is started by the leader and becomes contagious with members. Here is how it works. Wherever and whenever a leader sees a member or prospect of the Sunday School class or department he asks the question, "Will you be in Sunday School Sunday?" The response to the question comes from the member, and the leader says, "Good. I'll be looking for you." A contact has been made. This contact may be made with a chuckle or a smile to the member or prospect. It becomes a light and cheerful way of reminding the person of Bible study, and causes greater esprit de corps, the feeling of being a part of the group. The important thing is that the person is reminded of attendance in an unoffensive way.

This method is used when this leader sees his class members. The desired principle is to establish a mind-set with each member and prospect that causes him to think, *Bible study, Sunday morning, I should be there; I'm expected; I'm wanted; I'm needed; I'll be there.*

If a leader sees the same member four times in a week, and

asks the question, "Will I see you in Sunday School Sunday morning?" he makes four contacts. The point is not the number of contacts, the place of the contact, the style of the contact, or the time of the contact, but *the contact itself.* The number just reinforces the mind-set of continual thinking of Bible study.

What will develop is that the members will soon pick up the attitude and practice of the leader, to the place they will be asking the question of other members and will ask the question of the leader before he has time to ask the question. You may at first think the process silly, but when you realize it is a part in establishing a positive mind-set for growth, you will appreciate its value.

Another practice to further strengthen this mind-set is for the leader in a group meeting to make the statement to the group, "Are you all going to be in Sunday School Sunday? Good. Now I can put down fifteen contacts." All will laugh. The important thing is realizing each one in the group is reminded and confronted with the question and subsequent thoughts, "Am I going to be in Sunday School? I should be in Sunday School. I'm needed. I'm wanted. I'm expected. I'll go to Sunday School." When you study advertising in depth, you learn the first thing necessary to selling the product is determining the mind-set of the buyer.

In the religious world, I feel we must do the same thing. I think this concept gives us the fuller meaning of the Scripture, "Let this mind be in you . . . " (Phil. 2:5).

The mind-set of the members begins to change when they begin to think about Bible study on Sunday and making contacts whenever and wherever members and prospects are met. This action and process is the beginning of *Constant Contact Consciousness.*

To strengthen and perpetuate this thinking, a leader needs to ask for reports on Sunday of how many contacts were made last week. This reminds the members of whoever they saw, wherever they saw them, and the times they saw them, and of asking the question, "Will you be in Sunday School Sunday?" Those are contacts. They are important.

People have the habit of asking all kinds of questions when they meet friends. Why not make this question a part of the habit? This will help remove the guilt feeling of those who cannot and do not "door knock." This will cause some to use a method more comfortable to their own personalities for outreach. This will cause some to participate in outreach who would otherwise do nothing. This would give some a feeling of more worth in their Christian life and that they are doing something for the Lord.

Those of us who are leaders are often guilty of not providing a choice and variety of methods in outreach to the people. Providing these choices will cause more members to become involved in outreach. We need to broaden our mind-sets in making contacts with absentees and prospects using various ways according to people's own personalities and abilities.

Another misleading, narrow concept we as leaders have developed is the concept that visitation takes place only two hours a week. We have done this by giving recognition only to those people who actually knocked on doors between the hours of 7:00 and 9:00 PM on Thursday night. I feel this was done unintentionally, but the outcome can be destructive to our desired outcome and that is to reach people.

We need to develop a mind-set in the people we lead to think, "I'm responsible to reach people for Christ twenty-four hours a day, seven days a week, wherever I am, in whatever way I can, using whatever method is best suited to my personality and gifts."

I had an experience one day while coming across a discount store parking lot. One of my Sunday School class members yelled at me from three car rows away, "Hey, Neil, are you going to be in Sunday School Sunday?"

I yelled back, "No, I'll be down in south Alabama."

She answered, "That's all right. I want you to know I made my contact. See you in Sunday School when you get back." Now that was a mind-set developed for reaching people. That person developed the concept of thinking outreach twenty-four hours a day, seven days a week, wherever she was.

This mind-set was created because when I teach the class, I go down the row and ask everyone the question, "How many contacts did you make this week? What happened?" James 4:2b tells us "Ye have not, because ye ask not." If I don't ask the class members about making contacts, they're not going to tell me, and chances are they are not going to make as many. In all probability they are not going to think nearly as much about contacting. A mind-set of expectation and reporting has to be established. They have been conditioned to know that every time I see them, and it doesn't make any difference where they are, we talk contacts, attendance first, then about other things. They also do not want to come Sunday morning without some contacts to report.

Contacting Needs Variety

Visitation, the door-knocking kind only, to some becomes very dull. The same announcement from the pulpit about Thursday visitation soon falls on deaf ears. The following is a process that can put variety into the outreach of your church.

Now that we have begun to think of outreach in a broader sense, and we know basically the four different methods: door knocking, telephoning, sending postcards, and C. C. C. (constant class consciousness), the following process could be used.

The first thirteen weeks, recognize all types of contacts—door knocking, telephoning, sending postcards, and on-the-street contacts. List the names of people doing the contacting. Give the total number of contacts made that week. This is how the seven days a week concept is developed. Give recognition to all types of contacts, regardless of the day of the week the contact was made. Some people can telephone who cannot knock on doors. Some can send cards who cannot make other contacts. The goal is to bring about involvement of more people. Giving recognition motivates people. "Well done, thou good and faithful servant" (Matt. 25:21). Listing names will motivate others. As people see other people's names listed in the bulletin, they will say to themselves, "If they can do it, so can I."

There are at least three places names could be listed. (1) an insert in the Sunday order of service; (2) the weekly mailout paper; (3) workers' meeting promotion sheet. My personal preference is the Sunday order of service because more people will see it. Also recognition from the pulpit can be given.

The reason for taking this approach for thirteen weeks is to allow time for people to "catch on" to what is to be done.

After thirteen weeks, to give variety, change to the use of postcards only. Give recognition to those who sent cards, and tell how many cards were sent. Each card is a contact. Make this type of emphasis through all classes and departments of the Sunday School. Use this approach for contacts for eight weeks. A good time to use this emphasis is July and August because a general thought prevails that everyone is on vacation and therefore no one is at home to visit or call. Even if that were true, one thing is sure: they are going to come home some time. They will pick up the mail and find the card with your message.

When the eight weeks are up, go back to counting all type of contacts for another thirteen weeks. Since there has been another climate change, it is winter and bad weather sets in. So switch to the telephone during December and January for eight weeks. In some parts of the country where bad weather lasts longer, you may want to do this for thirteen weeks—throughout the winter months.

Most classes and many department's memberships could be contacted in thirty minutes or less. Ideally this should be done on Friday or Saturday evening about suppertime. Give recognition to telephoners who called and report on how many calls were made.

Using the above approach, these methods could cycle several times a year. This would not give the feeling to those who make contacts of doing the "same old stuff." It will involve others who have a reluctance to go "door knocking." So, ask the people to make contacts. Ask the people for a report of what happened and give recognition for services rendered. *Recognition* is the third vital part to making contacting a success. The first is the *assignment,* the second, the *reporting.* This will be discussed later in the chapter.

Using the telephone and card method of contacting can be calendared during periods of extreme weather conditions. As discussed before, the telephone can be used during nasty winter weeks and postcards during the hot summer weeks, when many are on vacation.

The strength of using a card for contact is it will catch up with the person eventually, whether the person is vacationing or not. He will know someone is thinking of him. A door-knock visit or telephone call many times is never noticed because the person is not there, but the card will convey the message, "Someone called." Please do not read into these ideas that I am for doing away with door knocking. It is an absolute necessity, as will be discussed later in the book.

Advantages of Using the Telephone

There are advantages in using the telephone. A telephone call will get inside of a house and out again, when a door knock will not always be answered. I've had this experience. I have knocked on a door, and I knew the people were inside. You wonder how I knew? As I was knocking I saw the curtain move at the front window. Now, dear friend, there's no wind inside that house to make the curtain move (unless there's a fan blowing). You know there had to be a person inside making the curtain move.

Some people don't come to the door for a number of reasons. It might be their house is a mess, and to some people that could mean embarrassment. So, they just don't come to the door. It might be there are beer cans around the room. They don't want to be embarrassed about certain people knowing their weaknesses. Or it might be they are not properly clothed, or their hair looks a fright. Whatever the reason, the door knock is not answered, and you can't make the contact. Incidentally, in some areas of the country, some people don't open their doors to anyone after 6:00 PM, no matter who it is. The telephone, however, can get in, leave a message, and be out in sixty seconds.

On Saturday night, I can call everyone in my class between 5:30 and 6:30 PM and find most of them at home, reminding them to be in Sunday School in the morning. This is in a sense a "last minute" reminder and a commitment of "Yes, I'll be there."

I am a strong believer in the work of the Holy Spirit. When out of town, I have prayed, "Lord, who needs a phone call from me today?" And God's Holy Spirit will send a name racing across my brain. I will make the phone call because of God's leadership to do so. I have been in California, Louisiana, Florida, Alabama, Arizona, or other parts of the country and made the phone call or sent cards. The interesting thing I have discovered happens on the other end of the line. The person was ready for and needed the call. God's Holy Spirit knew who needed the call. I have heard people in my class say, "Neil, the Lord must have led you because here is my problem. I needed your call. I appreciate you lifting me up in prayer."

Some of you skeptics may be thinking, *ridiculous*. But when was the last time you prayed and then moved at the direction of the impulse? Others of you may ask, "Who pays for the call?" I pay for the phone call. That is my decision, led by the Spirit. I don't run down to the church and say, "Church, re-imburse me $10.62 on my long distance calls this month." Nor do I subtract it from my tithes and offerings. No, that's my decision and joy. That's the way I believe the Holy Spirit is leading me. When you are led by the Spirit, cost doesn't con-cern you. Many business people in your church would have the same attitude. Give them the idea, and the opportunity to decide for themselves.

Some funny things happen using this process. Some of my class members have said, "Neil, where are you?"

"I'm in San Francisco."

Their reply has been, "Who's paying for the call?"

Laughingly I say, "I am."

"OK, I'll talk to you." They chuckle.

Here is a fact. Did you know there are certain times in a day you can call people for thirteen cents a minute? That's right, from 11:00 PM until 8:00 AM. One thing for sure, you will probably find people at home. The chances of missing them is far less. The important thing takes place: you left a message, which is, "I'm thinking about you; I'm interested in you; I'm praying for you."

So place emphasis on the *use of the telephone*.

Another fact: As I mentioned earlier, there are two times in the year when the weather keeps us from doing visitation. That's right, in the wintertime, you'll hear that "It's too cold, too dark, too dreary, too rainy, too sloppy, too slippery. It's the weather's fault whether I visit or not. Weather, weather, weather, whether you like it or whether you don't, I don't really care, but weather is my reason whether you like it or not. So I am justified by the weather not to make contacts." The other time of the year when the weather keeps us from visiting is summertime. "It's too hot, too humid, and the days are so beautiful. I have a boat and I love to fish. I love to play golf, camp, or a dozen other things. At any rate, nobody's at home anyway. Everybody is on vacation, so why do visitation? There's no need to do the visitation. Weather is the reason why we're not visiting whether you like it or whether you don't, whether you go or whether you won't. Weather is the problem whether you like it or not, so I won't, and I'm justified again by the weather." Great reasoning? Wrong!!!

It's time to change or use another type of contacting. In the wintertime when the weather is bad, concentrate on using the telephone. It doesn't matter if there are ten-foot snow drifts. The telephone can get through and into the house and leave the message. It's going to get through all kinds of bad roads and bad weather. The same thing is true in the summer. Eventually people are going to come home and pick up their mail.

Advantages of Using Postcards

Traveling as I do, living in motels, I have access to plenty of postcards. There is no problem in getting postcards. Other traveling people in your church have the same access to getting postcards.

I pray to the Lord and say, "Lord, who needs to hear from me?" Many times we make a mistake by sending cards to the absentees only. *One needs to write postcards to the faithful members also.* I say something like this: "Jim, I really count on you and depend on your being present. You mean so much to me in my teaching. I appreciate your faithfulness. See you Sunday, Neil. Prov. 3:5,6." You see, everyone needs a pat on the back and needs to feel wanted and needed. So be sure and contact the persons who are faithful. They need a pat on the back and encouragement. Let them know your need for them.

Sometimes I have a big time when I hand the clerk of the motel six, eight, or ten postcards. Every motel clerk is human, and I know that. After I've given one a number of postcards, the next day when I see him, jokingly I say, "Did you read my postcards?" And sometimes he will look at me, stammer and stutter, and mumble something. Well, you know, some do read the cards, because of human nature and time on their hands. They like to know what people say. This really came across to me one time when a desk clerk said to me, "Yeah, I read your postcards. What does this 'Prov. 3:5,6' mean?" He surprised me, so I said that it is a Bible verse that says, "Trust in the Lord with all thine heart; and lean not unto thine own understanding. In all thy ways acknowledge him, and he shall direct thy paths." Then I said, "Are you trusting in Christ? Are you letting Christ control and lead in your life?" You see, the fellow asked me about the verse, and what it meant. It is easier to make contacts and witness than some think. By the way, does it ever occur to you how many people might read your postcard before the person to whom you sent it reads it? The desk clerk, the postman who picks up the mail in the area, postal station workers, the postman who delivers it, and finally the person to whom it was sent all have a chance to read it. The post office says a minimum of seventeen people handle each piece of mail before it is delivered.

The Bible says, "My word . . . shall not return unto me void" (Isa. 55:11). So write a Scripture verse on the card. Use the cards at home or wherever you are. Begin now to broaden your mind-set and others you lead in the total area of contacting seven days a week, twenty-four hours a day, wherever you are, using as many methods as you know.

Advantages of Using C. C. C.

Going through the airport in Nashville, I saw Janet Kuka-meister, a security guard who checks everything you carry on the airplane. She and her husband were members of my Sunday School class. I said to her, "Janet, are you and Pete going to be in Sunday School Sunday?" She answered, "Yes, Neil, we are." I said, "Great, see you then! I've just made two contacts. That's one for Pete and one for repeat." She just laughed. Then I turned to the guard next to Janet and said, "Are you going to be in Sunday School?" She said, "I'm Catholic."

I said, "That's all right. Are you going to be in Sunday School Sunday?"

Then I turned to another guard and repeated, "Are you going to be in Sunday School Sunday?"

"I'm Presbyterian."

"Well, that's all right." I turned to the next. She responded, "I'm a Methodist." So here were a Methodist, Baptist, Presbyterian, and Catholic all working side-by-side. All were confronted with the question "Are you going to be in Sunday School Sunday?" When the question is asked, one must have to think, *Am I going to Sunday School? I ought to be in Sunday School. Why am I not going to Sunday School? I think I'll go to Sunday School.*

Getting someone to begin to think about attending Sunday School is the beginning of a completed act. I'm depending on the Holy Spirit to do the job of convicting and changing lives.

We often overlook the fact that these persons may have been wanting to attend a Sunday School but have never been asked. Regardless of what denomination they are, James 4:2b says, "Ye have not, because ye ask not." So ask!

With Janet, those questions did something else for her. She

later told me that after I walked away, it opened the door for her to talk about her Sunday School and church. "That's my Sunday School teacher," she said. "I would like to have you girls come with me to Sunday School and bring your husbands. He's a great teacher, and we have a great preacher. I'd like you to visit our class and church."

You see, it made it easier for Janet to make the witness after I was gone. She told me she had been wanting to invite them but didn't know how or the time did not seem to be right. My asking the questions opened the door.

About a week later, Janet saw me coming toward the security desk. I was about thirty feet away from the desk, and she yelled, "Neil, are you going to be in Sunday School Sunday?" And I said, "You got me! Yes, I'll be in Sunday School Sunday." She said, "I beat you. I asked first!!" Janet was thinking outreach. The mind-set had been established. Don't you know the other people in line waiting to go through security were wondering, *What are these people talking about, Sunday School?* I remind you again that whoever hears is confronted with the question and resultant thoughts, *Am I going to be in Sunday School? I need to be in Sunday School. Why am I not in Sunday School?* Hopefully he will think of going to Sunday School.

Think Sunday School. Think reaching people for Christ. Think contacts. When you think of visitation, think of expanding the concept to making contacts anytime and anywhere. Janet did.

Advantages of the Door-Knock Visit (Personal Visitation)

Door knocking is necessary. No growing church can live without it. A personal visit has the greatest strength in contacting because of the extra time, energy, and personal touch by the visitor. The one being visited subconsciously is aware of this fact. Deep down he appreciates the personal effort and concern of the visitor. The personal visit gives opportunity to talk about spiritual things more in depth than a card, telephone call, or light conversation on the street. Door knocking is an absolute if you want evangelistic growth to take place in your church. It is in the personal eyeball-to-eyeball contact that soul-winning is done.

Incorporate the four methods suggested above: door knocking, telephoning, postcards, and C. C. C. Broadening the mind-set on contacting involves more people, more days of the week, and more hours of the week. This allows people to use the method with which they feel the greatest ease.

Visitation Barriers Removed

Many people have mental barriers in visitation. We as leaders need to lead them to think positively. One way is to impress upon the persons doing the visiting that the person they are contacting needs Bible study so he can "grow in grace, and in the knowledge of our Lord and Saviour Jesus Christ" (2 Pet. 3:18).

When making contacts for the first time with a prospect, the visitor can make four simple statements:

1. I am *(his name)*.
2. I am from *(name of his church)*.
3. Are you attending Bible study anywhere on Sunday morning?
   (If response is "yes," commend them.)
4. (If response is "no" ask the following question: "May I invite you to attend and pre-enroll you in Bible study at our church?")

This simple outline can help many to know what to say at the door.

The goal of the visitor is to lead the prospect into attendance in Bible study. Many "would be" visitors have the fear they are going to have to "win the person to the Lord," and they do not feel equipped to do this. Consequently, they do not make contacts. If emphasis is made on motivating the prospect to attend Bible study and sharing with the prospect or absentee what Bible study means to the person doing the visiting, many of the fears of the visitor would be overcome and the visitor would start making contacts more readily.

Three Parts to Outreach

There are three parts to Outreach. The first part is *assignment*. We are pretty good at making assignments for people to contact. We will say, "Here's a prospect. Go see him. Here's an absentee. Go see her."

The second part of visitation is *reporting*. We are a little weaker here. We have different forms to use in reporting visits, but we really are not reporting them and using the information to the fullest once we get it. Some systems are reporting on an offering envelope. Some have it on a slip of paper. Some have it on a system called "Pocket and Card." There are different methods and systems. All are good. But no one is really asking for the reports and making use of them after the information is received. We make the assignments, but we don't ask for the reports and use the information reported to motivate other people. This is why in my Sunday School class, I periodically come down the row and ask, "How many contacts did you make? What did you find out?"

There have been several times when I didn't teach the lesson because in the reporting, a testimony meeting broke forth from what they found out. Those Sundays were probably some of the best Sundays in teaching they could have had—because the things that had been taught them all along had been put into action. If folks are not putting into action what you are teaching, then they may not be teaching effectively. Good teaching changes lives and becomes a part of the life-style.

So begin to ask for reports with expectation—"ye have not, because ye ask not" (Jas. 4:2b).

A state trooper I had in my class stands about six feet four and weighs well over 250 pounds. He is about "one axe handle" across the shoulders. He wears boots with a two-inch heel, and when he puts on his trooper's hat, he looks about nine feet tall. If he were to pull me over on the highway, step out of his patrol car, walk to my car window and say, "You were doing fifty-six miles an hour," I'd say, "Yes, sir, I sure was!" I wouldn't argue with him at all. However, he knows on Sunday morning I'm going to ask him, "How many contacts did you make?" And he's not about to say, "None." So periodically he will call me at 6:00 AM on Sunday morning and say, "Neil, are you going to be in Sunday School in a couple of hours? Just want you to know I made my contact. Bye, I'll see you." And he hangs up.

This is the only morning I can sleep until 7:00 AM, and he calls me at 6:00. It's my fault. He has been taught a life-style. I really don't mind how he does it or when he does it. A real joy comes from knowing he's doing it. It has become a life-style and a part of that class. That is one type of reporting.

For variety in reporting, sometimes for a period of time a sheet of paper is passed down the row. Contacts, whether they are door-knocking visits, telephone calls, postcards, or C. C. C., are recorded with the name of the member and number of contacts made. This indicates how many contacts were made during the entire week. See the various samples of forms that can be made and used for this purpose at the end of this section. You will see how this method broadens the concept of contact/visitation. It will go beyond two hours or one day a week. It will be twenty-four hours a day, seven days a week, using four different methods.

I would have thought a telephone operator would have been using the telephone extensively to do contacting. But because the leadership was making such emphasis on door knocking as the "only" method of making contacts, that was the only type she was attempting, and very little of that. She said, "It is very difficult for me to knock on a door and say something to a stranger face-to-face—partly because of my personality and partly because of my work schedule. I work 3 to 11 PM. But Neil, when you opened up this idea of using the telephone, it is so easy for me to do. I have no problems. I have been trained in how to use the telephone. Thank you, thank you, thank you." The interesting thing about using the telephone is that people will allow you to inquire into their personal lives over a phone. But when you're in their home, they're not about to let you see as much of their personal life. This is strange but true. Begin to use these other types of contacting and asking for the reports of phone calls, postcards, home visits, and C. C. C.

The third part to visitation is *recognition*. Remember, first we give the assignment of absentees and prospects. Next we do the reporting of what happened. And third, we give recognition. It costs so little to say "Thank you." One way you can give recognition to people who are doing the contacting is to have each person who made a contact to sign his name on a sheet. See the forms at the close of this section. Take the names and print them on an insert sheet in the worship hour order of service. You could title the sheet, "The Following People Made Contacts January 1—January 8." List their names. If you want to, separate them by departments or classes. However, *do not* put the number of contacts behind their names. A total by the class, department, or whole Sunday School could be included.

Do you realize an interesting fact: most people read every

word in the order of service. Do you know why? There are periods of time during the worship service when nothing else holds their attention. So they read every word. Knowing this to be true, we should put something in the order of service that will motivate and cause people to *want* to make contacts. When readers see certain people's names in the bulletin, they are going to say, "If they can do it, I can do it." That's the ultimate desire: *more involvement.* And it also says, "Thank you, thank you, thank you," to those who *are* making the contacts, and carrying the load. "Well done, thou good and faithful servant" (Matt. 25:21).

Anytime my name or picture appears in the Nashville newspaper, I buy ten newspapers. Do you know why? I have ten relatives, and I want them to know I made the newspaper. The newspaper is not interested in me personally. But the editors know human nature and that people like to see their names and faces in print. They are interested in selling newspapers. That is why part of the newspaper has sections in the sports, society, garden, obituary, *memoriams,* and so forth with all the names and faces. They print things that are going to sell more newspapers.

Well, dear friend, if it takes printing people's names in a bulletin to motivate people to make contacts, I'm going to print names. The Scripture says, "I am made all things to all men, that I might by all means save some" (1 Cor. 9:22). I can't win empty pews to the Lord. I can't teach empty chairs. I've got to have people. If printing names will get people into the church, let's print names. A preacher in southwest Georgia said, "Neil, my Sunday School attendance has reached 199 several times. Give me some ideas that will help me go over 200." So in jest I said, "Next time you have 199 in attendance, I suggest you open every door in the church and whistle for a dog. When he runs through the door, count 201. He has four legs."

I then said seriously, "Use the concept of making the assign-

ment, asking for the report, and *giving the recognition.*" The
first week he published six names in the bulletin. The second
week he published sixteen names in the bulletin. The third
week he published forty-eight names in the bulletin. The third
Sunday he had 252 in Sunday School. It will work. So work
it. Think of the different ways to strengthen the outreach with
these three parts—assignment, reporting, and recognition.

If space is not available in the order of service, list names in
weekly mailouts to church families, or in the Wednesday night
workers' meeting sheet, or make a visitation poster and place
in a high traffic area of your church listing the names of those
making contacts for the week. The following forms will give
you the names of those making the contacts. You may want
to color code each form to help people be conscious of a different emphasis in contacting.

Visitation with a Balance

There is a balance to visitation that needs to be kept in
mind. Too many times we contact the same group of people
when we need to have a balance. It seems like many of us
only go after the absentees. When you only contact the absentees, you will not have growth in your class, department, or
Sunday School. In contacting, about 80 percent of the contacts should be with absentees, 15 percent with prospects, and
5 percent with a view of soul-winning. This will give good balance for growth. If the concepts of using the telephone, writing
postcards, talking to members on the street are used, 80 percent of contacting absentees can be done on Monday, Tues-
day, Wednesday or any day of the week. If you want growth,
keep in mind a *minimum* of 15 percent of the contacting time
should be used for reaching prospects. When you come to visitation day, the door-knocking visitation should be *concen-
trated on prospect visitation*—not absentee visitation. Generally speaking, the most doors one can knock on on visitation

Constant **C**ontact **C**onsciousness

As You Go

Note:

t your own copy

d art work here.

Yes, I was a part of the team this week!

Date   Name   Number of Contacts

Total Number of Contacts   _____

Number or People Making Contacts _____

Use this form for thirteen weeks, encouraging all types of contacts being made: door knocking, telephone, postcards, and C. C. C.

Constant Contact Consciousness

Note:

Put your own copy
and art work here.

Make a Personal Telephone Call

YES, I was a part of the team this week!

Date	Name	Number of Contacts

Total Number of Contacts _____

Number of People Making Contacts _____

Use this form for eight weeks, usually winter months—
December and January. Some areas of the country where bad
weather is longer you may want to use this form for three
months.

Constant Contact Consciousness

Note:

Put your own copy

and art work here.

Send a Personal Card
or Letter

Yes, I was a part of the team this week!

Date   Name   Number of Contacts

Total Number of Contacts   _____

Number of People Making Contacts   _____

Use this form for eight weeks in the summer months, July and
August, or for three months if you choose.

Constant Contact Consciousness

Note:

Put your own copy

and art work here.

Ring Doorbells
and visit prospects one by on

Yes, I was a part of the team this week!

Date	Name	Number of Contacts

Total Number of Contacts _____

Number of People Making Contacts _____

Use this form for four weeks prior to a high attendance campaign or revival. The idea is to knock on every member's door or prospect's door, leaving a flyer of the emphasis you are in.

night is about three, and one of those will likely not be at home. But leave a card so that a contact is made. A person can visit only two, possibly three houses on visitation night.

If one concentrates all of his time contacting the absentees, no growth will take place. Therefore, on the day of visitation, concentrate all of the time toward *prospect* visitation.

There should be a certain amount of the total time of contacting given to soul-winning. This will be about 5 percent. A person should pray to the Holy Spirit and ask his guidance to give wisdom as to who needs to be approached about accepting the Lord. God will give guidance as to time, place, and what to say.

Four weeks before a revival, make a concerted effort for a personal visit to every member and prospect of the Sunday School class or department promoting attendance at the revival. To the lost, present the plan of salvation, and try to win them to the Lord, or make a definite effort to get them to the revival. A simple soul-winning system is in the last chapter of the book. All teachers and workers of the Sunday School can use it.

Using these percentages as a guide, 80 percent with absentees, 15 percent with prospects, 5 percent toward soul-winning, you will achieve a balance in contacting and growth in your Sunday School. Visiting an absentee on visitation day is done when the class member has not been present for four straight Sundays. If telephone contacts, postcards, or talking when seeing such a member on the street isn't getting him there, then a personal visit is necessary. Something is wrong, spiritually, and this person needs that personal face-to-face contact.

Outreach Organized

There should be an outreach leader for the entire Sunday School. This leader has the responsibility of leading each department to organize for visitation and to give guidance to the outreach program of the Sunday School. There should be an outreach leader for each department of the Sunday School.

If a Sunday School does not have departments, but is a class Sunday School, there should be an outreach leader for every class of the Sunday School.

The Adult and Youth department outreach leader has the responsibility of leading each class to elect a class outreach leader and of leading the classes in the department to make contacts.

The responsibility of an Adult class outreach leader is to organize the class members into groups of five to eight and lead them to elect a group leader. The group leader has the responsibility of contacting absentees in that group and leading members of that group to visit prospects and absentees.

Each group leader and outreach leader should not only give assignments for visitation, but ask for reports on the results of the assignment.

Visitation for Special Emphasis

Periodically, it is good to have an all-out thrust for visitation when every member and prospect is contacted. Special days, revivals, and high attendance weeks should be emphasized. These emphases give a boost to the whole church program. These types of emphases can only be done about once a quarter or twice a year to be effective. It cannot be continued week after week. A "contact" blitz emphasis on a weekend when every member and prospect has a contact from someone in the class is an example.

Visitation by Two's

Here is another ongoing, effective growth idea. In one of the earlier segments about visitation I wrote that visitation seems to take a nose dive in the summertime and again in the wintertime. One way to keep door-knocking visitation high during those times is for the Sunday School director, or in a larger church the department director, to go to every class and department and ask, "Who is going to represent this class this week in growth visitation? I need two people." In smaller churches it could be one person, depending on the size of the class or department. The goal is to have every teaching unit of the entire Sunday School organization represented on visitation day. Again I remind you, this may not be your style. But you can catch the concept and adapt it to your style.

The first time I used this idea was a number of years ago when I was minister of education at First Baptist Church, New Orleans, Louisiana. I would go through some of the Adult departments and classes on Sunday morning and say, "I need two names from each class for visitation. Who are they going to be this week?" I came to one of the Senior Adult classes and the teacher said, "Neil, you are disturbing my teaching."

I said, "Dear teacher, if your class is not putting into action what you are teaching, you may not be teaching effectively."

She quickly said, "All right, I'll be one. Vice-president, you be the other." She had the ability aggressively to tell people what to do and they would. She really wasn't sold on the summer visitation by two's idea. But I got two names from her class.

The next week I came by her class and said, "Who is going to represent your class in visitation this week?"

She said, "You again?"

I said, "Yes, ma'am, I'm going to be here every week all summer long because this is our emphasis: 'Every teaching unit represented in visitation.' "

She turned to two of her members and said, "All right, you and you." Again, she had the personality to make demands of her class members and get a response. That is what you call "aggressive leadership." I think everyone could be more aggressive in the Lord's work. The third week she could hear my heels clicking as I was coming down the hall to her room. A sheet of paper shot out from underneath the door, and there were the two names. I just stood there and laughed to myself and thought, "Ye have not, because ye ask not" (Jas. 4:2b). Don't be afraid to ask and *expect*. This is "Visitation by Two's." This will carry you through those hot summer months or those cold winter months.

Visitation—"Ye have not, because ye ask not."

Many people do not make contacts because we as leaders have not asked them to do so, or we ask but do not expect them to do so, or fail to ask for a report and give them recognition. We have become our own enemy. The person doing the visiting can develop an attitude that says, "The leaders really do not care what happens in visitation because they never asked what happened," or, "The leaders don't care because they never say 'thank you' for what I do." Leaders need to keep in mind that Christians are human and need compliments, recognition, and praise. It is not too much to ask or give to people who give freely of their time, their energy, and their money. Now don't get pious on me, especially you who are paid staff members of a church and say, "They should do it because they love the Lord." How much would you do for free? We are paid to do what we do. The least we can do is say "Thank you." Give the people who do the job a "Well done, thou good and faithful servant" (Matt. 25:21).

Visitation Methods and Materials

There are at least a half dozen different methods and materials for visitation. The latest simplified method is the Pocket and Card system that can be purchased from the Materials

Services Department at The Baptist Sunday School Board, Nashville, Tennessee. For many years churches have used Form 120. If these are working effectively for you—stay with that system. Whatever materials and methods you use, be sure you understand fully what it is designed to do, and work its design to the fullest.

A Visitation Chorus

To the tune of "He Keeps Me Singing" (Chorus—"Jesus, Jesus, Jesus . . .).

> "Visit, Visit, Visit—Every Absentee
> Visit Every Prospect—That's the Way to Victory."

This is a great song to sing before going out to visit on Thursday night. It lifts the spirits, and gives a positive mind-set and sense of victory in the heart of those going out.

Hopefully, this section has provided you with interpretation, inspiration, and motivation for contacting people.[1]

Note

1. Words and tune SWEETEST NAME, Luther B. Bridgers, 1910. Copyright 1910. Renewal 1937. Broadman Press. All rights reserved. *Baptist Hymnal,* 1975, p. 435.

Notes and Thoughts

4

Ideas for Growth

Analyzing Your Sunday School to Make It Grow

How many times have you asked yourself, "What does it take to grow a Sunday School?" If you are worth your "salt" at all, you are constantly asking yourself this question and looking for an answer.

Every church and Sunday School is in a (1) *growth,* (2) *maintenance* or (3) *decay* status. There are certain percentages and ratios that are indicators to help the leadership decide which of the above states their Sunday School, department, or class is in. The following becomes a guideline to move from a maintenance or decay status toward a growth status.

Let us start with the basics in analyzing where your Sunday School is and then seek to discover the weak areas that need strengthening or special help.

If your average attendance in youth and adults has dropped below 50 percent in attendance and 70 percent in the Preschool and Children's areas, you probably have problems in one or more of four areas of emphasis. These four areas have strong influence in having a successful growing Sunday School. The four areas are:

1. Visitation
2. Training

3. Organization
4. Space

Visitation: What kind of a visitation program do you have—weekly or "weakly"? Is there a variety or choice for making contacts or is there door knocking only? Are other opportunities of contacting available, such as telephone, cards, and C. C. C.? Is contacting encouraged seven days a week, anytime of the day? A growth status would be indicated by having every teaching unit represented in visitation each week. Less than this indicates a maintenance or decay status.

There are three types of visits or contacts. (1) Contacting *absentees* is maintenance. (2) Contacting *prospects* is growth. (3) *Soul-winning* is growth. These types of emphases will vary from week to week. The variety of visitation has been discussed in an earlier chapter.

Training: When was your last study course to improve the level of teaching? January Bible Study or a Vacation Bible School study course does not count. We mean an age-group study—"working," "understanding," "teaching," "reaching," or books of comparable emphasis. The latest books in my denomination are the "Basic" Sunday School books. If you are providing two or fewer such type study courses for each age group a year, you are probably in a maintenance or decay status. If you are providing three or more a year you are in a growth status.

Organization: Are your classes and departments within their proper enrollment size? When an Adult class has fifteen to twenty on roll it is probably in a growth status. Twenty-one to twenty-five indicates a maintenance status, and twenty-six or larger a decay status. Other age-group classes and departments have maximum enrollment sizes. See age-group division books for these formulas. There are other factors that have influence on the above: space, class organization, teaching quality, and so on. More about pupil/worker ratio later.

How well are the departments and classes organized for outreach? Does each department of the Sunday School have an outreach leader? Does each Adult class have an outreach leader? Is there a group leader to encourage attendance for every five to eight people enrolled in each Adult class? Five to six members in a group indicates growth; seven to eight indicates maintenance; above eight indicates decay.

Are the leaders trained in what is expected? Are they given an opportunity to function and report each week? An excellent book to use to train outreach leaders is *Training Outreach Leaders for the Sunday School,* written by T. Frank Smith.

Space: Does each department and class have adequate space for growth? It takes ten to twelve square feet of floor space for each person in attendance in a department or classroom for youth and adults. It takes twenty-five to thirty square feet of floor space for preschoolers and children in their departments. You may have the best trained workers, the best department and class organization, the best visitation program, but if you have inadequate space, *you cannot succeed* in increasing attendance.

Double whatever the maximum floor footage allows in attendance. This will tell you what your effective maximum enrollment can be for the class, department, and total Sunday School.

Remember: *The building (space) in a large measure controls the program.* A space analysis will let you know where (age groups) you can have growth. It will let you know when you need to add (build), acquire, or adjust the present space to continue to grow. Twelve to fifteen more square feet per person in attendance allows for growth; ten to eleven indicates a maintenance status; fewer than ten promotes decay. People will not attend as often when each is allowed less than ten square feet of floor space—except for funerals and Christmas programs. They will endure being crowded for a short period or a one-time only situation. No one, however, likes to be in an overcrowded classroom for an hour. People will grade themselves by not attending.

Now that you know the general guidelines for analyzing your Sunday School, where would you say your weak spots are? Where would you say your needs for emphasis ought to be in the whole Sunday School and in each department: visitation, training, organization, or space?

Departments and classes will differ one from another as to needs and sometimes from the whole Sunday School. The above method allows you and your leadership to pinpoint the specific and immediate needs, thus deciding on priorities.

Raising the Attendance

The attendance of a Sunday School will always be a fairly fixed percentage of the enrollment. One rarely ever hits 100 percent of the enrollment. Nor can it be maintained for any length of time. Therefore, to increase the attendance, one must increase the enrollment. It is that simple. There is a direct relationship between the attendance and enrollment. When enrollment goes up, so does attendance. When enrollment goes down, so does attendance. You can rant and rave about being more perfect in attendance, but you can get only so much out of people. What we need to do is go out and get more people to increase the enrollment.

How do you increase the enrollment? The open enrollment concept is one way to do it quickly. This open enrollment concept states that a person can be enrolled anytime, anywhere, as long as he agrees. The prospective "enrollee" therefore does not have to be within the "four walls" of the Sunday School class to be enrolled. He does not have to attend three Sundays before he is asked to enroll. He can be enrolled anywhere, anytime when he agrees.

With the above concept in mind, the following is a list of the ways the Sunday School enrollment can be increased by using the open enrollment concept. This list is by no means all the ways enrollment can take place. There are others that you will develop on your own as you put these into practice. Pick out several from the list you know will be accepted immediately by your congregation and concentrate on them for several months. After these have been proven successful and established, pick several more. You will see the enrollment increase. Also, the attendance will increase. When the Sunday School attendance increases, so will the offerings, worship attendance, and baptisms.

A way to use the following form effectively is to go through the list crossing out those methods that absolutely would not be applicable in your area or situation. Delete them from the list. A word of caution—don't delete too many.

Make a number of copies, distribute them to your workers, asking them to check the five methods they feel would be the most effective ways of enrolling people. Have them return the forms. Make a composite tally sheet of the number of people who thought the statement had a strong possibility of increasing enrollment. This way the Sunday School workers will identify the top five that have priority. However, this does not eliminate those ideas that some people thought were valid. All ideas could be used by someone. If people have input and choose a method, they in a sense commit themselves to that method.

Twenty-five Ways to Grow (using an open enrollment philosophy)

Check the ones you can do *NOW*

___ 1. Have pastor and staff members carry enrollment cards as visits are made (to newcomers, church visitors, hospitals, and other pastoral ministries).

___ 2. Inform new church members they are enrolled in Sunday School, Church Training, Brotherhood, or Baptist Women.

___ 3. Place enrollment cards in pew racks. (a) Invite people to fill out the card and place it in the offering plate. (b) Suggest that members take cards with them and enroll people through the week.

___ 4. Clip an enrollment card to each prospect slip sent out for visitation.

___ 5. Monthly or quarterly, go door-to-door in specific selected areas (Mini-action).

___ 6. A month prior to each revival, have a major thrust to enroll people.

___ 7. Clip enrollment cards to the front of each class record book.

___ 8. Have "Greeters" carry enrollment cards and enroll people as they come through the church door.

___ 9. On special "choir" programs, VBS parents' nights, high attendance times, and revivals, call attention to the enrollment cards in the pew.

___10. Give several enrollment cards to new Sunday School and/or church members and urge them to enroll friends and family members.

___11. Have the pastor enclose a return addressed enrollment card in his letter to Sunday visitors.

___12. Have Cradle Roll visitors carry enrollment cards and enroll parents in the homes.

___13. Use the VBS Transfer Plan (pupils).

___14. Conduct parents' visitation following VBS to enroll them.

___15. Have bus ministry workers enroll parents of children coming on the bus.

___16. Conduct a direct mail program, a three- or four-letter campaign about Bible study. Enclose a self-addressed enrollment card in the final two letters to: (a) newcomers and prospects; (b) church members not in Sunday School (quarterly).

__17. Use the Adult Start-A-Class plan.

__18. Stand at the back of the auditorium and enroll early comers to the worship hour.

__19. Have the pastor call church visitors and enroll them over the phone Sunday afternoon.

__20. Give enrollment cards to all visitors of weekday activities.

__21. Give enrollment cards to apartment dwellers and ask them to enroll persons in their apartment house or complex.

__22. Have college students take enrollment cards and visit in the dormitories or at BSU events and enroll students.

__23. On the "first" visit of a person to a class or department, present an enrollment card instead of a visitor slip.

__24. Have people who fill out visitor slips in the worship hour write the words, *"Enroll me"* across the top of visitor slip.

__25. Conduct a direct mail campaign to the unenrolled parents of children in your Sunday School to ask them to use the enclosed enrollment card to join an Adult Sunday School class.

How to Enroll People in Bible Study by Telephone

Reasons for enlisting by phone: Using the telephone to enroll people is faster than other methods. It allows people who have physical limitations to perform a ministry in the church. Telephones can make contact with people who are reluctant to come to the door. Telephoning can gather information in a short period of time. Telephone contacts can be made in the evening when most people are home. Telephoning is great for public relations. Telephoning lets people in the community know of your church and location. Telephoning says someone is interested.

Enlist the Telephoners

These are the people who are going to do the calling of the prospects. They can be any age, youth through senior adults. It is best that youth call youth and adults call adults when assignment of the prospect cards is given.

The number of the cards can range anywhere from twenty to twenty-five cards per telephoner. This is approximately one hour of work.

Special Note: All conversations over the telephone are basically the same. However, there is a recognizable difference in each conversation according to the type of prospect being called. Each conversation must be used specifically with the type in the list it is identified with. The third statement in the telephone conversation is different in each list and is marked with an asterisk.

If, after the four basic statements are made, a person says yes to the question, "Can I enroll you?" the caller then fills out an enrollment card for the person he is speaking with. Generally when you enroll one member of a prospective family you can enroll the entire family on the one call. Thus the next question after the enrollment card is filled out is, "Can I enroll other members of the family?" If, instead, the person says no to the question, "Can I enroll you?" the telephoner says politely, "Thank you for your time. Come visit us at *(name of church)* sometime. We would like to have you. Good-bye."

List #1—Instant Prospects: Morning Worship Service

Place a 3″ x 5″ card in the back of the pews. During the announcement period of the morning worship service ask the people in the congregation to take one of the cards.

Now that they have the cards in hand, ask them to write the name of one person they know who is not in Bible study anywhere on Sunday morning. That person may be a friend, neighbor, coworker, schoolmate, relative, or the person himself sitting in the congregation, waiting to be asked.

This process was discussed in detail earlier under the subject "Instant Prospect."

The person doing the calling would say:

1. "Hello, I'm *(name of caller)*."
2. "I'm from *(name of church)*."
3. "Your friend *(name of person who gave the information)* gave us your name and said you were not attending Sunday School Bible Study anywhere."
4. "Could I enroll you in Sunday School Bible Study with your good friend, *(name of person giving information)*, right now over the telephone?"

List #2 — Church Members Not Enrolled in Bible Study

To prepare this list one would take the church roll and compare it with the Sunday School Adult roll. Names that do not appear on the Sunday School roll are prospects and should be listed with their phone numbers.

This is a list the pastor uses to enroll people in a pastor's class. However, all churches do not have a pastor's class or several other Bible teaching programs listed below. Therefore, the telephoners could enroll people in one of the areas of Bible teaching their church does provide. Listed below are nine areas of Bible teaching a church could provide.

A person can be enrolled for Bible study in at least one of the following areas:

1. Pastor's class
2. Regular Sunday School class or department
3. Homebound ministry (for those physically unable to attend)
4. Cradle Roll (newborn babies in the community)

5. Sunday workers' class (usually held on Wednesday night)
6. Special Education (for retarded)
7. Language class
8. Class for the deaf
9. Students away (college students or professionals out of town)

If there is a need for a class not offered by your church, consider starting one at once. Most of the enrollment will be in one of the first three areas.

The person doing the telephoning would say the following:

1. "Hello. I'm *(name of telephoner)*."
2. "I'm from *(name of church)*."
3. "You are a member of the church but not enrolled in a Sunday School Bible study class."
4. "Could I enroll you in a Sunday School Bible study class right now over the telephone?"

If the person says he is an invalid, shut-in, or mentions some other similar circumstance, ask to enroll him in the Homebound ministry.

He may say he can't come because he works on Sunday. Ask to enroll him in the Sunday workers' class that meets on Wednesday night.

Look at the nine possible alternatives to lead a person to be enrolled in one of these areas.

List #3 — Unenrolled Parents of Children and Youth in Your Sunday School

The way you discover parents not enrolled in Bible study is to list the names of all children in Preschool, Children, and

Youth departments. Compare this list with the adults who are enrolled in Adult Sunday School Bible study classes. If a parent's name is not on an Adult Sunday School class list, add it to a list of these parents with their phone numbers.

The person doing the telephoning would say the following:

1. "Hello. I'm *(name of the telephoner)*."
2. "I'm from *(name of church)*."
3. "Your child is enrolled in our Sunday School. We see you are not enrolled in a Sunday School Bible study class. We have excellent Bible study at our church."
4. "Could we enroll you in a Sunday School Bible study class, right now over the telephone?"

List #4 — Sunday Visitors in the Worship Service or Sunday School for the Past Six Months

Make a list of the visitors who gave an address in your town or community. Put the phone number along with the name.

The person doing the telephoning would say the following:

1. "Hello. I'm *(name of the telephoner)*."
2. "I'm from *(name of church)*."
3. "You visited our church recently, and we were glad to have you. We have excellent Bible study classes on Sunday morning."
4. "Could I enroll you in a Sunday School Bible study class, right now over the telephone?"

A practice that a church can use is to register every visitor for whatever activity is being held at the church. Examples are Sunday worship service, Wednesday prayer series and activities, Easter and Christmas cantatas, VBS commencement, recreation activities, and any other special activities or occasions your church may be having. This gives you added prospects for the above list.

List #5 — Present Prospect File

Make a list of all prospects with their telephone number.
The person doing the telephoning would say the following:

1. "Hello. I'm *(name of telephoner)*."
2. "I'm from *(name of church)*."
3. "We understand you are not attending a Sunday School Bible study class anywhere. We have an excellent Bible study on Sunday morning."
4. "Could I enroll you in a Sunday School Bible study class right now over the telephone?"

List #6 — Newcomers to Town

The utility companies (telephone, gas, electric, and water) and real estate brokers have a list of families who have moved to a new address.

Make a list of the names of these families with the phone numbers.

The person doing the telephoning would say the following:

1. "Hello. I'm *(name of the telephoner)*."
2. "I'm from *(name of the church)*."
3. "We understand you people have just moved to that address. We are happy to have you in our community. We have an excellent Sunday School Bible study class on Sunday morning."
4. "Could I enroll you in a Bible study class, right now over the telephone?"

List #7 — Cross-Reference Telephoning

To make this list you must have access to a cross-reference telephone book. In the cross-reference phone book you can find your section of town by streets. A cross-reference will give you the streets and house numbers with the names of the people who live at that address in your church community.

A *Special Note:* Because of the time between when the information was gathered for the cross-reference book and the time you use it, the information may be approximately 80 percent accurate. A new cross-reference book is anywhere from six to twelve months old the day it is delivered to you. Don't be discouraged. It is a way to find prospects.

The person doing the telephoning would say the following:

1. "Hello. I'm *(name of the telephoner).*"
2. "I'm from *(name of the church).*"
3. "We see you are living in our church community. Are you attending a Sunday School Bible study class anywhere? If not, we have an excellent Bible study class on Sunday morning."
4. Could I enroll you in a Sunday School Bible study right now over the telephone?

List #8 — Apartment-Complex Residents

A suggestion: Mail a promotional piece about your church to all the apartment complex residents before you call to indicate someone will be calling soon.

The telephoner would say:

1. "Hello. I'm *(name of the telephoner).*"
2. "I'm from *(name of the church).*"
3. "Did you receive a letter telling about our church? Are you in a Sunday School Bible study class on Sunday morning?"
4. "Could I enroll you in a Sunday School Bible study class right now over the telephone?"

List #9 —

Encourage all members to make a list of their own relatives, neighbors, friends, and persons with whom they work, and turn this information into the church office. This process is similar to *List #1*.

Using any or all of the above will add people to your Sunday School roll. Additional specialized lists can be thought of and added.

Remember, "Ye have not, because ye ask not" (James 4:2*b*). Start asking!

How to Enroll People by Mail

Much can be done by mail. If this were not true most businesses would be out of business. They are very dependant on the mails.

Churches also can do much to reach people by mail.

Following are samples of four letters that can be used to reach people. The same sample response card can be used with each letter.

The way to make something good better is to change it to fit your church and the way you would say it. Therefore, write the sample content so it sounds like you. Remember the *pastor* is the most *powerful person* of *promotion*, so these letters should come from his desk.

Sample Letter 1

To Church Members Not Enrolled
In Sunday School

Dear (Name of Church Member):

According to our record you are a church member but *not* a member of the Sunday School Bible teaching hour.

In 2 Timothy 2:15 the Bible says to "study to show thyself approved unto God. . . . "

There are many other Scriptures that indicate we are to gather for fellowship, Bible study, and spiritual growth.

We believe the born again Christian can and will want to do this for God's glory. We believe this can be done by joining the Sunday School.

There are a number of areas a born again church member can join in Bible study.

On the enclosed card are a number of options a church member can choose from to be a part of the Sunday School Bible teaching program.

We want you to "grow in the grace and knowledge of the Lord Jesus Christ."

Please indicate your choice and return the card.

Your pastor,

(Pastor's name)

Sample Letter 2

To Unenrolled Parents of Enrolled Children

Dear (Person's Name):

We are delighted to have your child in Sunday School Bible study. We believe you are doing a great thing in encouraging your child to study God's Word. The Scripture says, "Train up a child in the way he should go: and when he is old, he will not depart from it."

We believe you can strengthen the training greatly by being enrolled in a Sunday School Bible class, too. This could be very meaningful. In Timothy chapter 4 we find the words, "Be thou an example."

In our Sunday School Bible study program we have a place for everyone.

Enclosed is a mail-back card for you to indicate your choice of where you would like to be enrolled. Return the card so we can get your study material to you.

Prayerfully yours,

(Pastor)

Sample Letter 3

To Visitors At Church Services and Sunday School

Dear (Name of Visitor):

We were glad to have you in our services.

We want you to be more than a visitor. We want you to be a member of our Sunday School Bible teaching program.

Enclosed is a mail-back card for you to indicate in which part of the Sunday School Bible teaching program you would like to be enrolled. Please return the card so we can get your Bible study material to you.

We believe everyone should be in some type of Bible study.

See you Sunday in Sunday School Bible teaching hour.

Yours for Bible study,

(Pastor)

Sample Letter 4

To Prospects

Dear (Name of Prospect):

We understand you are not enrolled in Sunday School Bible study anywhere.

We believe everyone should be in Bible study somewhere. We want you to be enrolled with us.

There is a place for you.

Enclosed is a mail-back card with a number of choices for you to choose.

Please indicate and return the card so we can get your study material to you!

We will be looking forward to seeing you Sunday.

Prayerfully yours,

(Pastor)

Sample Copy

Mail-Back Card

Please check one of the following places you would like to be enrolled in Sunday School Bible study.
__1. Regular Sunday School
__2. Pastor's Class
__3. Homebound Ministry (those who are shut-ins)
__4. Cradle Roll (for newborn babies or expectant mothers)
__5. Special Education (class for the retarded)
__6. Sunday Workers (those who work on Sunday morning; class meets Wednesday night)
__7. Language Class (ethnic groups)
__8. Deaf Class
__9. Students Away (college or professionals out of town)
Return the mail-back card or call the church office to notify us of your preference.

Special Note: The mail-back card will have to be adapted to the areas of Bible study you offer in your church.

Other Types of Letters That Build a Church

1. Letters to potential parents (Cradle Roll prospects)
2. Letters to masses in a community to find prospects
3. Follow-up letter to respondents of the letter above
4. Letters to enroll all shut-ins
5. Letters to youth (student body of high schools)
6. Letters to ethnic groups (for a new ethnic class)
7. Letters to parents of children with special education needs (retarded)
8. Letters to members asking for leads to prospects
9. Letters for Sunday School visitation
10. Letters for High Attendance Days or other special days
11. Letters for stewardship commitment
12. Letters for potential workers
13. Letters to potential bus riders
14. Letters to the faithful (appreciation)
15. Letters to apartment complex dwellers
16. Letters to those in a hospital
17. Letters to those in jail
18. Letters to the newcomer to town
19. Letters for those who have a crisis (source newspaper)
20. Letters to bereaved families (source: newspaper)

You will think of others as you become more involved in direct mail ministries.

Quarterly Enrollment Activities

To make a Sunday School and church grow, there is a constant need to work on increasing the enrollment. Listed below are ways to increase the enrollment.

ACTION: Once a year, canvass several days to enroll new people and find new prospects from a given area of your community.

MINI-ACTION: Once a quarter or twice a year, canvass on one day only, either Saturday afternoon or Sunday morning.

SATURDAY MORNING TEAM VISITATION: Visit church members not enrolled in Sunday School, or visit visitors to the church service not yet enrolled.

VBS TRANSFER PLANS: Visit or telephone within three days after Vacation Bible School is over.

REVIVAL CONTACTS: Follow-up done within thirty days of the revival.

NINE WAYS TO ENROLL BY TELEPHONE: (Details in previous section).

CLASS/DEPARTMENT GOALS: Establish outreach goals by class or department.

ONE-FOR-ONE: Personal goals given to outreach leaders and teachers.

FELLOWSHIP BIBLE CLASS TRANSFERS: Enlist members of home Bible study classes for church classes.

CHURCH MEMBERSHIP HUNT: Enroll church members not presently enrolled in Sunday School.

PROSPECT ANALYSIS AND ASSIGNMENT: (Member/Prospect matchup).

NEIGHBORHOOD OUTREACH TEAMS: Organize outreach teams by neighborhood.

INTERNAL CENSUS: Once a year, unenrolled parents of children enrolled in Sunday School; church members not enrolled.

WEEKDAY SUNDAY SCHOOL: Have Sunday School during the week for those people who work on Sunday.

ENROLLMENT IN SUNDAY SERVICES: Have enrollment cards in the pews.

USE OF THE TWENTY-FIVE WAYS TO ENROLL IN SUNDAY SCHOOL: (details in previous section).

SPECIAL EDUCATION EMPHASIS: Once a year in September

LANGUAGE GROUP EMPHASIS: Once a year in September

DEAF MINISTRY EMPHASIS: Once a year in September

BUS MINISTRY: Enroll families of bus children in Sunday School at least once a quarter.

SHORT TERM: Outreach Task Force to visit all persons listed on prospect forms.

CRADLE ROLL CONCENTRATION

BABY HUNT: Spring and fall emphasis.

HOMEBOUND HUNT: Emphasis twice a year—winter and summer.

WEEKLY CHURCH VISITATION: Visit weekly for enrollment.

Notes and Thoughts

These Are Serving

A silent motivational tool to lead people into service can be used in an Adult classroom. Make a wall chart of poster board. Put the heading, "These are serving." List each class member or former class member's name and the place each is serving in the church. For example: It may be "Jim Smith, usher"; "Tom Jones, fifth grade teacher"; "Jane Jones, Acteen leader." Giving recognition of service will motivate. Recognize people, and it will cause other people sitting in the class to begin to think of service and places they can serve. It will promote the mind-set of service.

When the different types of services are recognized along with the people who are serving in those positions, the class member will begin to think, "If they can do it, so can I." Thus, when they are asked, their mind-set has already been conditioned toward service. It is a compliment to the teacher when he is leading in the direction of service. The proof of good teaching is to see how many times you have multiplied yourself. "By their fruits ye shall know them" (Matt. 7:20).

The church is forever in need of small jobs, such as building a bookcase, painting a wall, making a chalkboard, making a bulletin board, changing light fixtures, repairing a crib, fixing a broken chair, etc. The list can go on and on, and is almost endless. These are generally short-term tasks that someone needs to do. But in the present process, many things go unmentioned and undone.

The following process could solve some aspects of this problem, shorten the time tremendously, and provide many opportunities of service for people within the church. Remember, part of the secret of success is involvement. Place a bulletin board in a high traffic area, which most generally is near the church office, in the hallway. Title the board, "Service Board."

Instruct all people who are workers in the total church program that whenever there is need in a class or department or anywhere in the building they should take a blank 3″ x 5″ card and write the need and the name of the person who has the need with the phone number to contact. Place the 3″ x 5″ card on the "Service Board." From the pulpit (the most powerful place of promotion), or in the Sunday order of service, mention from time-to-time the opportunities of service that are posted on the bulletin board. It may be good to mention some of the needs from the pulpit.

"Ye have not, because ye ask not" (James 4:2b). Many people do not serve—not because they don't want to—but because they don't know what is needed, are never asked or told where they could serve. For instance a worker may need a cabinet or a shelf or a table for an interest center, book center, or music center. Placing the need on the board will allow those who could make these items aware of the need. Many times there are people in the congregation who can make items like these and would be happy to do so without cost to the church. This can become their opportunity for other needs to be made known within the church and could be communicated to various committees, personnel, or other leadership involved. However, the service board's primary function is to draw people into short-term service who many times cannot or will not do other things or serve in places of leadership. Involvement is a key to success.

An interesting thing about this process is that the time element is shortened between the request and the delivered service, with little disruption to a large number of people. The joy also is that another person has had an apportunity to serve in a special way with the "gift" or talent God has given him. The more ways the congregation is involved the happier the spirit of the church.

Furniture Talks

The furniture can tell you what the members in a class or department expect.

It can tell you what the class concept of growth is.

It can tell you the class expectations for new members or visitors.

It can tell you who is absent and needs to be contacted. It can tell you the maximum enrollment for that class or department.

It can tell you when to create new units.

It can tell you when you need to move to a larger space.

Furniture talks. Listen to it.

Why is it in an Adult class that has twenty people on roll, there are only ten to twelve chairs in the room? The furniture is saying, "Only half of you come. The other half stay at home. Don't bring visitors or ask people to join the class. We would have no place to seat them. After all, this class is for our *four*, no *more*. Don't change the *score*. We don't want any *more*. Don't be a *bore*. So shut the *door*." The furniture indicates "We do not believe in growth. We do not believe in visitation. We do not believe in change. We do not believe in Acts 2:47: . . . 'And the Lord added to the church daily . . . .' "

In the above illustration the furniture is speaking negatively. There is a need to change so that furniture will speak positively.

If a class believes in growth, at least twenty-one chairs should be in the room for an enrollment of twenty. The furniture will tell you when to create a new teaching unit. If twenty-one chairs won't fit in the room, move to a larger room or create a new teaching unit. If you want to grow you need adequate space.

The time to initiate the idea of furniture talking is on Sunday morning. Each teacher or worker should have available a number of felt-tipped markers, a roll of masking tape, and a supply of 3″ x 5″ index cards, enough to exceed the Sunday School roll by one or several more chairs.

As the members arrive for class give each one a card, a marker, and some masking tape. Ask each to write his first and last name in block print. Then ask him to write his phone number under his name on the card. Have the member place the card on the chair back with the masking tape.

Those members who are absent should be contacted. When they come, have each fill out a card and tape it on the chair.

After a certain period of time (two to three weeks), for those members who have not attended make cards with their names and phone numbers and tape each 3″ x 5″ card to a chair. Now twenty members have their names on a chair.

The one or two extra chairs should have cards that say, "New Member." This encourages enrollment on the first Sunday a visitor comes. It also is a silent motivator to reach people.

The reason for having each class member write his name and tape it to the chair is that the act itself becomes a motivator for participation, awareness of a place, responsibility to attend, and it creates a number of other low-key influences for attendance. Use this method only now and then. It visually lets the class know how many people really are members of the class.

The quarterly is a contacting tool.

At the close of the class the teacher or outreach leader can say, "Turn to next Sunday's lesson. Look around the room and see what chairs are empty and who is absent. Write down two names of absentees and their phone numbers in the quarterly. This way when you study your lesson this week, you will be reminded to give the absentee a call."

The advantage of this process is that several people may contact the absentee instead of only one. Also people do not lose their quarterly as often as they do a slip of paper in the pocket.

Now the furniture is speaking positively. It is saying:

- "There's a place for you."
- "You are expected."
- "We believe in growth."
- "Look who is absent."
- "Visitor, join our class today."
- "We have space for more people."
- "We are not a social clique."
- "We believe in reaching people."
- "It is time to create a new unit."

Alternate ideas or options: In churches where a double Sunday School is operated use two 3″ x 5″ cards side-by-side of different colors with a #1 or a #2 in the upper corner to indicate which class the member belongs to.

In some classes and departments where it is not feasible to use the cards on the chair back an alternate plan can be used. Place names and phone numbers on 3″ x 5″ cards. Inside the door on a wall two columns could be posted—one for those *present*, the other for those absent. When a person comes through the door he could move his card from the absent column to the present column (or this could be done by a worker in a Children's department). At the close of the class period the teacher or worker calls attention to the absentee column and asks everyone to write two names and phone numbers on their quarterly lesson and give each a phone call next week. Encourage children to do this. We are building a mind-set in a child to think growth and outreach.

Furniture does the talking. Listen to it!

Don't Use Visitor Slips in the Class

"WHAT?" you say.

Has it ever occurred to you that visitor slips may be considered by some as rejection slips? To many first-time attenders the visitor slip can give a negative impression. The first-time attender is considered only a visitor. The impression can be given that the class is not ready to accept him as a new member. The first-time attender can get the impression that the class wants to try him out for awhile and see how well he attends, what kind of a person he is socially, and whether they want him in the group.

Of course, no one in the class makes such statements to a person who attends the first time. Yet that is what might go through a first-time attender's mind when he is handed a visitor slip. Ideally, if growth is the attitude of the church the first-time attender should be given an enrollment card and invited to fill out the enrollment card. "We are glad to have you. We want you in this class."

Another element in the process that we may not be aware of is that we have taken church doctrine and lowered its importance—and raised Sunday School doctrine above church doctrine. Let me illustrate. Say I'm in your Sunday worship hour and the preacher preaches a sermon, gives an invitation, and I walk down the aisle the very first Sunday I'm there. I take the pastor by the hand, make my profession of faith, or come into the fellowship of the church by transfer of letter or statement of the fact that I belonged to a church that is no longer in existence. The church accepts me with open arms.

Some pastors would give me a hug, shake my hand, and tell me how glad they are to have me in their congregation. Some people in the church may even become a little emotional about my coming and cry over me. The pastor asks everyone to come up front and give me the right hand of Christian fellowship, rejoicing over the decision I have made to come into the church fellowship. I may even receive a free ticket to Wednesday night's supper meeting if the church has that type of program.

But what happens if I walk into the same church's Sunday School class? Class members look at me. Maybe someone speaks to me. But the tones of their voices are questioning who I am, what my intention is, whether I will come into the class and maybe create a little bit of a problem for them. Many more feelings are communicated silently when I walk into the Sunday School class. How many times have you experienced this type of feeling? Was there ever a time when you walked into Sunday School class and a person asked you to fill out an enrollment card the very first Sunday you attended? Believe me, it is a rarity for that action to take place in the average church.

Many times, Sunday School classes are reluctant to put a person on the roll for fear that person will "pull down their percentage." We must keep one thing in mind. It is not a grade we witness to. It is people we witness to and win to the Lord.

When we practice a process of waiting for a person to attend three Sundays or more before we ask them to enroll, we have just elevated Sunday School doctrine higher than church doctrine. This is wrong. The church has priority in doctrine over Sunday School. Often it is much more difficult to become a Sunday School member than a church member. This thought does not occur to many Sunday School leaders.

A practice needs to be established that when a first-time attender walks into a Sunday School class, he is automatically given an enrollment card and asked to fill it out. If the person is truly a visitor, he will tell you. Then cross out the word *enrollment* and write the word *visitor*.

Let me illustrate with an example from business. When a person walks into a store to buy clothes, a well-trained salesperson does not say, "Do you want to buy a suit?" The store has established a mind-set in the salesperson's mind that the customer is there to buy. So the question "Do you want to buy a suit" has already been answered. The salesman assumes that is why the customer is there. The salesperson has only four things he needs to discover to make the sale. One, the size. Two, the color. Three, the style. Four, how much money the customer wants to spend. A good salesperson always asks questions that lead to a positive answer and to the final sale.

We as workers in a Sunday School class should take the same attitude and approach. A positive growth attitude to take in Youth and Adult classes is to assume that every person who comes to class wants to become a member. The first-time attender is given an enrollment card and asked to fill it out. Sometimes the way a question is asked indicates our negative expectation, for example: "You *don't* want to join our Sunday School class today, do you?" You can see the reaction of the person being asked when the word *don't* is used. Take the positive approach by saying "Please fill out this enrollment card."

Using the positive approach method gives the feeling of expectation. It gives a feeling of total acceptance and that the class wants the first-time attender to be a part. Many first-time attenders have come for that purpose. The information is taken, and the first-time attender becomes a part of the Sunday School class and department immediately.

A positive mind-set for growth should be kept—even if the first-time attender says, "I'm just a visitor."

The next statement, a positive one, might be, "Well, where do you live?"

"I live twenty miles from here."

A positive response should be, "That's all right, come on and enroll! You have just a little farther to come than the rest of us."

Think positively. Think growth.

You see, with the mind-set of outreach, a person keeps in mind that the newcomer was able to be in attendance on this morning. If the newcomer feels total acceptance, he will get there again in the weeks to come. *Distance is not nearly so much the problem as is acceptance.*

To establish this mind-set in a Sunday School, consider removing all visitor slips from the record boxes and using enrollment cards for four to six weeks. People are all creatures of habit, and our habit has been to hand a person a visitor's slip the first time he walks into a class. Regardless of how many times you tell your workers to use enrollment cards, they will continue their old habit of giving the individual a visitor's slip if they are available. It is like being on a diet. You have to take all things that you should not eat on a diet completely out of sight. Otherwise, you will fall back into your old ways. So to change your Sunday School workers' habits, remove all visitor slips. If a person is truly a visitor, then simply scratch out the word *enrollment* and write the word *visitor* across the top of the slip or card. This process needs to be done for four to six weeks. It takes time to break a habit. It takes time for people to catch on to why you are using this process.

This concept was presented to a group of ministers of education at an assembly. One minister of education thought this was the worst idea he had ever heard. He thought I was as wrong as wrong could be for even considering such a thing. Before ninety-two other educational directors, he verbally "nailed me to the wall." This does not bother me a bit for I know where I'm going. I know how to grow a church. The problem was that the young minister of education really did not know where he was going nor how to grow a church.

The thing that pleased me was that the man had an open mind. It is great when an individual has an open mind and is willing to try an idea. About four weeks later, I received a letter from him. He had tried the method. His comment in the letter was, "Neil, in one day we enrolled thirty-six people using your suggested process of removing the visitor slips. I want you to know, we enrolled more people in one Sunday than we have enrolled in the past three months. Thanks! It works."

It does work if you will work it. "Ye have not, because ye ask not" (James 4:2b). Ask people to enroll.

Notes and Thoughts

Stars and Bars for Attendance

Here is an idea many churches are using to reach people and motivate people to attend. There are some educators however who feel this is a low level of motivation.

As you read, you decide if these ideas are for you and your congregation.

The Stars

There is a need to commend, encourage, and lead people to participate in perfect attendance at Sunday School. This can be done by giving recognition to those who are perfect in attendance.

Do you remember when some of you were children in Sunday School? The teacher had your name on a wall chart. A star would be placed behind your name every Sunday you were in attendance. It was always a thrill for me to know I had accomplished something. Some people feel that people should not receive awards but ought to attend because they love the Lord. This is true. I don't deny that concept. But I also know that people have a need to be recognized. Many need to have a pat on the back or some recognition. We should recognize this need. Most members are still babes in Christ. We think they should react as full-grown Christians. Some are not even Christians. So give recognition, a pat on the back.

The idea of stars on a wall chart can be used with children, youth, and adults. The pastor of a major church in southern Mississippi, when I shared this idea, said, "I intend to start this idea next Sunday with my pastor's class which meets in the chapel."

Several days later I shared the same concept in an associational meeting with a group of Sunday School leaders in a south Mississippi town. One of the ladies said, "I teach the

TEL class. Everyone has to be sixty-seven or older to be in my class. This is a great idea, and I intend to start next Sunday with my class."

With the above in mind, decide whether or not your class would accept this idea. Remember, you never know until you try.

A strong positive advantage in using this idea is that the outreach leader can point to the wall chart and quickly say, "Look and see who is absent. When you see them this week, remind them they were missed at Sunday School." This fits beautifully with the C. C. C. concept discussed earlier.

The best illustration I know happened to me in First Baptist Church, Weatherford, Oklahoma. The children's workers, during our conference, made the wall charts. They were to be used on the next Sunday morning in a department.

I cautioned the workers on Sunday not to affix the stars themselves, but to let each child place his own star. Where this idea has been used in the past, many workers want the wall chart to look nice and neat, so *they* place the stars on the chart. It is easy to tell when a worker has placed all the stars. The stars are all placed so neatly. They are centered in the square by the name, and the points of the stars are all pointing in one direction. But allowing the child or class member to place the star gives him a feeling of accomplishment.

The Sunday morning I was in the Weatherford church, a child, who was about seven or eight years old, was given the star. He marched across the room showing all the other children his star as he walked to the wall chart. He made one more turn as he got to the wall chart to see if everyone was watching. They were. He then began to lick the back of the star. I thought that child had licked enough times to lick all the "stickum" off, but he placed it on the chart, and with his clinched fist, pounded three times with a big proud grin which expressed, "Look what I've done." Then he marched back to his seat. He felt his accomplishment. It is important that people, especially children, feel they have made accomplishments. The attitude today is so strong to negate everything and everyone, especially children. Some children get little or no encouragement or feeling of accomplishment. If the church does not give affirmation to people, who will?

I imagine that the following Sunday morning, that child got out of bed and said, "Mama, hurry up. We don't want to be late. I've got to put my star on the chart for perfect attendance. Mama, have you ever gotten a star for anything?"

Dear friend, there is no question that this is teaching the importance of attendance. The book of Proverbs says, "Train up a child in the way he should go: and when he is old, he will not depart from it." Attendance to hear and learn God's Word is important.

Perfect attendance pins can be given at the end of three months, six months, nine months, one year, and each year up through forty-one years.

The Bars

Remember also when you were a child, how some churches gave attendance pins for recognition annually to people who had perfect attendance? Then there came a period when many church leaders made fun of this practice, intimating that it expressed a low level of motivation. Consequently, the incentive for being in perfect attendance was killed. Many churches quit giving pins and bars for perfect attendance. An interesting observation is that attendance and growth dropped off during those years. Has it ever occurred to you *why* some people made fun of those who recognized perfect attendance in this way? The reason could be that the ones making the remarks were not perfect in attendance and could only justify themselves by joking about this method of motivation. It is possible some leaders committed an error during that period in history. A number of Scriptures can be given. Christ himself said, "Be ye therefore perfect, even as your Father which is in heaven is perfect" (Matt. 5:48). And certainly Paul made reference to consistent attendance in the book of Hebrews when he said, "Not forsaking the assembling of yourselves together, as the manner of some is" (Heb. 10:25). If you want to grow, begin next quarter encouraging perfect attendance. Encourage all those present to be committed to perfect attendance. You could begin to build perfect attendance between now and the beginning of the next quarter. Special recognition could be given to all who are perfect in attendance the next quarter.

There is a perfect attendance pin for three months, six months, nine months, and, each year. Each year a bar can be added or exchanged, indicating the number of years of perfect attendance. It is possible to receive perfect attendance bars for forty-one years.

During the worship hour on Sunday morning the pins could be presented by the pastor to every person who was perfect in attendance.

I can hear immediately the skeptic saying, "That would take away from the worship hour." Instead, the presentation can be a meaningful worship experience. I remind you again of Paul's statement in Hebrews, "Not forsaking the assembling of ourselves together." What better recognition could motivate others to be perfect in attendance? This is an accomplishment. "Well done, thou good and faithful servant." If people are not doing what is being preached and taught, then there may not be any real preaching or teaching, for preaching and teaching changes life-styles. If there is no change in life-style, there has been no effective preaching or teaching. People have to *hear* the word to "grow in grace, and in the knowledge of our Lord" (2 Pet. 3:18). If people are not coming they are not hearing.

Another motivating factor comes into play when we give recognition. People see other people receiving recognition.

Some will say, "Why, if that person can do that, so can I. Therefore, I will try, also." This could be a way we can lead one another by our lives.

I believe this could be one meaning of what Paul was talking about when he said, "Present your bodies a living sacrifice, holy, acceptable unto God" (Rom. 12:1).

People are to "grow in grace, and in the knowledge of our Lord." If they are not present in the worship services it is doubtful that they are doing much growing in the grace and knowledge and understanding.

If it takes a star or a pin or a bar to motivate people to attend so they might grow, I will gladly give the star, pin, and bar. A number of churches have begun to use these ideas and are showing immediate growth, numerically and spiritually.

I Will Commit to Be Faithful

Here are three ways to institute a perfect attendance program in your church:

Example 1. In the worship hour, after preaching a sermon on commitment to being faithful, distribute 3" x 5" cards printed with the statement, "I commit to thirteen weeks of perfect attendance." After a word of explanation and signing ask the people to place the cards in the offering plate. For the next thirteen weeks the pastor makes reference to the commitment and gives recognition to those who are still perfect in attendance. At the close of the thirteen week period those perfect in attendance receive the three months Sunday School perfect attendance pin. Other services will be affected by this commitment. These cards can be posted in a highly visible traffic area of the church during the thirteen weeks. Visibility gives recognition and motivation.

Example 2. A second example is to print the card with the statement, "I commit to perfect attendance for the next thirteen weeks." Design the outer edge of the card listing each

Sunday with a date. When the person comes to Sunday School, punch his card. Each person fills out his card and keeps it in his Bible, bringing it each week to be punched. The pastor, as on the above plan, comments and encourages attendance.

Additional recognition can be given by collecting all the cards at the close of the thirteen week period. Post them on a bulletin board in a high traffic area of the church. Display them for four weeks. Group them by those who were 100 percent. Next, group those who were between 80 to 100 percent. Third, group those who were between 70 and 80 percent. You may grade them differently.

The punch card idea works very well in a bus ministry. The bus driver can punch the cards as the people get on the bus. Therefore, take the idea, adapt it however is best to fit your particular program and choose the method that suits the personality of your church.

A church in Nashville used this method during January, February, and March. The pastor said, "This is the first time we have averaged over two hundred in Sunday School in January, the first time we have averaged over one hundred in Church Training, and the first time we have averaged over fifty on Wednesday night." Saying thank you and giving recognition does help attendance.

Saved to Serve, Not Sit

As we teach and preach, we need to look at each individual in our class or congregation and pray to the Holy Spirit for guidance. Ask him to show us or make us aware of what each individual could do for the Lord. I know this process will work. When I teach or preach, I look at individuals and pray this prayer, "Dear Lord, what can this person do for you? How can he serve?"

Let me illustrate: When I was seventeen years old, I had

won several solo voice contests in the Indiana State Music Festivals. Someone said to me, "Neil, have you ever thought of using your voice for the Lord? You could be a wonderful testimony for him."

No, it had never occurred to me that I could use my voice for the Lord. It took that person planting an idea in my mind that I could be used for the Lord in some way in music, if I would but let him. As a result, I actually began my ministry for the Lord in the music field. It was because someone made me aware of an ability and talent I had. As I grew older, other people would indicate through their preaching, or in a direct communication, other talents that could be used for the Lord.

As leaders we can be very influential in leading people into greater service by indicating to them abilities and talents we see they have and encouraging them to use those talents for God's glory. Remember, God uses what we have when we try.

The problem is that many people are not aware they have some abilities or talents. Using this concept will lift some people to service who might otherwise never be used. It also can become an affirming ministry that "someone sees an ability and has confidence in me." It is good to know that someone feels you have value. This helps that person feel a sense of worth and of being needed and important. This is one area where some of us as leaders are weak, the area of "lifting up the saints" and "encouraging one another."

Let me be quick to state that I know everyone cannot teach, preach, sing a solo, play an instrument, direct music, or pray in public. An attitude some have is that if a Christian cannot do one or more of these six major things, he is not much as a Christian. That attitude is wrong. What we need to do as ministers and leaders is lead people to find their places of service in a church regardless of how important or unimportant others might feel the job is. We must help people find and fill their places of service and do it to the greatest of their ability.

Let me give you an example: If you held a gun to my dad's head and said to him, "Neil, pray in public or we are going to pull the trigger," he would say, "I cannot pray in public. Pull the trigger."

If you said, "Neil, we want you to teach a Sunday School class or we are going to pull the trigger," he would again answer, "I cannot teach. Pull the trigger."

"Neil, we want you to sing a solo."

"Pull the trigger."

"Neil, we want you to play an instrument."

"Pull the trigger."

There are some people who would think my dad is not much of a Christian because he can't do any of these major things in the church. Some would think he's not much. Well, that is simply not true. When you read the New Testament, you find throughout that God gives different people different talents, different abilities, and consequently different expectations. We read in Paul's writings, "some, apostles; and some, prophets; and some, evangelists; and some, pastors and teachers" (Eph. 4:11).

Not all of us are saved to serve in the same capacity. Let's go back to my dad. In his church there is not one door hinge that squeaks. You see, he goes around oiling all the door hinges. There is not one electrical outlet that does not work. He takes his electrical testers and makes sure they work. If they don't, he fixes them. There is not one light bulb that is burned out or flickers in the main auditorium or in classrooms. By the way, have you ever tried to preach or teach with a flickering light bulb? I mean, there is no way that you can preach with real consistency when you've got a light that goes flick, flick, flick, flick. Have you ever tried to lead music when the light is flicking one rhythm and you are trying to sing another rhythm? The restrooms are always clean and never lack for the necessities. He always makes sure they are ready. The snow is shoveled off the sidewalks and salt sprinkled Sundays and Wednesdays in the winter. In northern Indiana there is a lot of snow. In the summer, the grass is always mowed, and the yard looks attractive. Allow me to state here that my dad is *not* the janitor of the church. But he feels this is something that he can do and does well. This is his ministry. These are not the kinds of jobs that one gets accolades for, praises, or a "Well done, thou good and faithful servant" publicly from the pulpit. I doubt seriously if many people in my dad's church know that he is the one who takes care of all of the above items mentioned and more. The most obvious service my dad performs is that some Sundays he passes out the order of service and receives the offering.

My concept of service is that God looks with favor upon a person like my dad who serves and serves well to the best of his ability. His service oils the wheels of God's kingdom, and the work can continue forward smoothly because the hinges are oiled, the lights are working, the snow is shoveled, the grass is mowed, and the rest rooms are cleaned. Those things are just as important to God's kingdom as is preaching from the pulpit. No job in God's sight is too small. Again I remind you of Paul's statement that, "We are labourers together." Some plant, some water, some cultivate, "but God giveth the increase." Therefore, when we preach and teach, let us look at each individual. Let us help him find his place of service beyond the major five or six places we generally look and think.

Incidentally, when the church my dad and mom attend and are charter members of was getting ready to purchase ground and build in the 1940's, the board of trustees went to the bank for a loan. Names of men of the church were given to the bank to ensure the loan. One name given was a Sunday School teacher. The bank officer refused his name, saying "He went bad on a personal note." A man who could pray beautiful prayers so eloquently was refused. The bank said, "He is not a man of his word." My dad was the only name they accepted. My dad is not a wealthy man, but he has something some people don't have. The banker said, "Neil Jackson is a man of his word. We know by experience." In Proverbs it says, "A good name is rather to be chosen than great riches" (Prov. 22:1).

Periodically, in the Sunday School class I teach, I will make the statement, "You are saved to serve, not sit. If you stay in my class longer than three years there is one of three things wrong with you. One, you are dumb. A great motivator once said, 'Tell people they are dumb, and that will motivate them to move.' Two, you are lazy. That same great motivator made the statement, 'Tell a person he is lazy, and that will motivate him to move—slowly—but he will move! The third possibility is that you just really don't want to do what God wants you to do. You are saved to serve, not sit."

After I'd made that statement one Sunday, at the close of the class, one of the members said, "Neil, do you know what I got out of your teaching today?" I said, "No, tell me." She said, "One more year to sit in your class." I laughed. She had gotten the message. That's a great attitude. At least they are catching the concept. They know there is a time limit on sitting to learn. There are so many places and jobs in a church where people can serve.

Using the broadest concept of service, we can find a place of service for everyone. However, the real key to this concept is praying for the leadership of the Holy Spirit to guide us as to what ability each person has, and what job he could do in the church. Here is an idea that can lead a number of people much like my dad into service.

Welcome 7

This idea was picked up from a church in Hattiesburg, Mississippi. They have a practice by which every person who comes through the door of their church gets his hand shaken at least seven times before he sits down in a chair in a classroom. I asked the question, "Why seven?" They indicated that is the number of perfection. I was quick to reply, the number three is also a perfect number. If by chance you are in a small church, you could use the same idea with the concept of three handshakes before a person sits down.

The church in Hattiesburg has a group of people organized very much like the ushers for Sunday services. They call it the "Greeter's Committee." The Welcome 7 greeters have a chairman who enlists the number of people needed to carry out the activity. They have two people stationed at every outside entrance to the entire church. Because their church is large, they have two people on each floor down the long hallways. They have two people inside each department, and one person inside a classroom. These greeters come fifteen minutes early to Sunday Shool. They take their assigned stations, and each person who walks through the door or down the hall into the department gets a handshake and hears the statement, "Welcome, we are glad to see you. We are glad you came to study and worship with us today." Of course, the statement varies from one person to another.

The Welcome 7 concept involves a large number of people in service each Sunday. The chairman of the Welcome Committee circulates through the building to see if any place is vacant. Immediately a substitute is put into service.

An interesting thing happens in this process. Most of us are creatures of habit who walk through the same door every Sunday morning. In fact, most of us park in the same parking spot every Sunday. The reason is we come at a certain time each week. The parking lot is partially filled about the same way each week. Therefore our customary spot is generally still open. We also have a habit of parking on the same side of the church and going in the same door each Sunday. Because of this habit, the greeters soon know the regular members. It is easy for them to spot a visitor. The question can immediately be asked, or the statement made, "We are delighted you are visiting us today. Could I show you to a class or department? Would you please fill out this enrollment card?" A number of things can be said to the newcomer at that moment. Whatever is said is decided by the practice of the particular church. It is important for people to feel welcome, wanted, and appreciated. It is important for members to feel they have a service. It is important to God's work.

Count the number of entrances your church has. Multiply by two. Then count the number of Youth and Adult departments you have and multiply by two. Count the number of Youth and Adult classes you have. Multiply by one. Add the number of people necessary to have two in long hallways on first, second, or other floors. You can see quickly how many people are needed to carry out the concept of Welcome 7 in your church. It is a place of service, and every place of service is important.

About fifteen minutes after Sunday School starts, all of the greeters move to their regular classrooms, since their ministry has been completed. An alternate idea is to have a Sunday School just for the greeters. Their ministry is just as important for that thirty minute period as is the teacher's for another period. The initial contact is many times the lasting impression your church makes upon the visitor. Therefore, let us make it the best we know.

If your church is small, you could have Welcome 3 as your practice. You would have two people at the outside entrances and one person inside the classroom. This will work. Work it!

Notes and Thoughts

Deacons Who "Deac"

This idea comes from a church in Shreveport, Louisiana. The Sunday I was visiting there, there were approximately eight hundred people in the early worship service with fourteen deacons serving as ushers. The 11:00 AM hour had approximately one thousand people in attendance, and a different group of fourteen deacons served as ushers. During the "Welcome" visitors cards were passed out. The people were asked to give complete information concerning their address, and then drop the card in the offering plate. After the offering was received, all of of the visitors' cards were removed from the offering plate. Any cards indicating a Bossier City or Shreveport address were divided equally among the fourteen deacons who served at that worship hour. Sunday afternoon, between 1:00 PM and 5:00 PM, these deacons knocked on the doors of the visitors who attended services that morning. They gave the visitors a packet of material with information about the total church program. A family census card was filled out. If a person was not at home, the packet of material was left hanging on the doorknob with a card from the deacon saying, "Sorry we missed seeing you today. We would be happy to have you as members of our church. We will be looking forward to seeing you in the evening service and next Wednesday."

That evening, before the Church Training period, the deacons who made contacts that afternoon met with the pastor giving the information they had discovered. Monday morning, a letter was sent from the pastor indicating his joy in having the visitor in the services. He personalized the letter by saying he was happy "Deacon Jones" was able to visit their home Sunday afternoon. (This gives recognition to the deacon making the contact.) He invited them to be in attendance Wednesday evening. Enclosed were guest tickets to Wednesday night supper.

The only suggestion I would add to the above process is for the deacon to ask the visitors if he could enroll them in Sunday School Bible Study right in the home where he is visiting. This uses a growth mind-set of enrolling anyone anywhere as long as he agrees.

The thing that impressed me in the above process was the immediate follow-up of the visitors. This says to the potential new member that this is a church that is aggressive and interested in reaching people, the kind of a church he is looking for. It also indicates that this is a group of deacons who "deac."

Finding and Enlisting Potential Workers

Workers are a constant need for any church. Most churches look for workers in Adult classes only. Many nominating committees establish barriers against finding potential workers that eliminate a number of good leadership possibilities.

Several recognizable barriers are: "How faithful is this person in attendance?" "Is he a tither?" "How much training does he have?" "We need a worker of a particular age." And so the list goes on and on.

More potential workers can be discovered by looking at the church roll, not the Adult Sunday School roll only. One loses sight of many people who could be good workers or have been workers in the past. They have dropped out of Sunday School for various reasons. The reasons for dropping out are many—the challenge is lacking; there is boredom; there is no involvement; or some other "legitimate" reason.

We lose sight of people because they are not actively in Sunday School. Many people attend the worship services only. These people are potential workers.

A fact that is generally true and difficult to realize is that if your church is over ten years old, over 50 percent of your resident members are not enrolled in Sunday School. The overwhelming majority of this group are adults. They are your potential, unchallenged leadership.

It is no wonder that 20 percent of the congregation is carrying over 80 percent of the church load. We have not asked 50 percent of the people to become involved. James 4:2b states, "Ye have not, because ye ask not." Therefore, take the entire church roll. Name by name, ask two questions. *One,* Could this person do a job in our church if he would?" Do *not* think of a particular job. You are preparing a list of potential workers only, not considering a specific place of service.

If you can say, yes to the above question, then ask question number *two*. "Would the church accept this person as a worker?" If you can say yes to these two questions, you have just found yourself a potential worker. Put the person's name on the list of potential workers.

The problem of most nominating committees is they want a worker to be perfect in all ways before being considered. We forget where we were in our religious life when the Lord found us and started using us. We forget how *he* has had patience, love, understanding to get us where we are. And remember, we are still a long way from being perfect. Therefore, let us not overlook the potential in people. Also, do not leave out the leadership of the Holy Spirit to guide us to people and develop them, "in grace, and in the knowledge of our Lord and Saviour Jesus Christ" (2 Pet. 3:18).

You will discover you have a list of potential workers that is beyond your initial thinking and needs.

Once you have gone through the entire church roll (which will include the names enrolled in the Adult classes), you now have an entire list of potential workers. You are ready to enlist and train workers.

Option 1: Workers needed for a particular age group:

Step 1: Pray to the Holy Spirit and say, "Lord, who on this

list should work with this age group?" One by one look at every name and consider the person emotionally, spiritually, physically, educationally. Is he a potential worker for that age group?

Step 2: When an impression (leadership of the Holy Spirit) comes to you as you look at the name, write it down on the list of needs.

Step 3: You have gone through the entire potential worker list considering each name. You now have a list of potential workers for a particular age group.

Step 4: Pray for the leadership of the Holy Spirit for one name to fill each vacancy in the age group. Do not have two names for one vacancy, as this weakens the enlisting power. Using this method, the person doing the enlisting can say with all honesty, "You are the only one. The Lord led us to you." Enlisting these people for a worker-training class should be done using a one-on-one method of approach also. Your conversation to that person would be as follows:

"Mr. Smith, the Lord has led us to you. We want you to be involved in a worker-training class for eight weeks (length of time should be given). We meet on Sunday morning (specify time and place) during the Sunday School hour. We believe you can be used of the Lord in a mighty way of service with this age group. (Identify the age group you desire him to work with.) We want to help you be prepared. Will you do what we believe the Lord wants you to do?"

Adapt the above conversation to your own style of conversation. Catch the concept. Keep enlistment on a spiritual level and a "you are chosen" level, not on an "anybody can do it" level. That is a low motivational level.

Option 2: Smaller churches that need only one or two workers for an age group would enlist people to be trained as a worker in the Sunday School. You would use the same enlistment process as above with a slight change. That is, encourage the prospective worker to study the book for the particular age group by home study. Or if you have four or more workers for several age groups, you can teach the book *Basic Sunday School Work*, by Harry Piland, for general Sunday School information, using the above Sunday morning format.

Option 3: Use the list for other worker needs in Church Training, Baptist Women, Brotherhood, the Music Ministry, and for finding outreach leaders, pianists, secretaries, department directors, Sunday morning greeters, and so forth. For any place of service in your church for which you have a need, you now have a ready-made source to draw from. Keep the concept in mind, "Everyone is saved to serve—somewhere, not sit. Let us as leaders, help them to find a place of service."

Five-Week Worker Training

Every church is in constant need for trained leadership.

Every church has some kind of method for enlisting workers.

Every church varies in its method. One extreme is "shoving" a quarterly into a prospective worker's hand and saying, "You teach next Sunday. Do the best you can, and we'll be praying for you. God bless you." And that is the extent of training and praying for the new worker.

The other extreme is a continuous training program that never puts a person in a place of responsibility.

Here is a plan to give the prospective worker a foundation, orientation, experience, and an option to find the age group he is physically, spiritually, emotionally, and educationally best suited to serve, according to his skills and temperament. The program would last five weeks.

We will assume the Lord has led us to a prospective worker. As a Sunday School director or minister of education, your end of the conversation may sound something like this:

"Jim, the Lord has led me to you to be a worker in the Sunday School. I believe you would be an excellent worker with adults (give age group you think the person is best suited to work with). Your personality and other abilities have much to influence that age for the Lord. If we give you training for five weeks, would you say yes to the Lord, for that age group, and begin the training program this week? Here is what you can expect. This is the study course book, *Basic Adult Sunday School Work* (or a similar teacher-training book for the age group). Here is a sheet of questions taken from the book. (The questionnaire is made from the questions or statements from the back of the book and is prepared by the local church). Jim, take about two weeks to read the book and answer the questions with an open book. When you finish, return the book and questionnaire to me. (See sample of questionnaire at end of this article.) Jim, I will meet with you next week to see how you are doing in the study of the book, and discuss with you any questions you may have. Starting next week, on Sunday, I want you to visit the Adult department for department openings and to be in Mr. Smith's class as an observer of his class for the next two weeks. Attend weekly workers' meeting with Mr. Smith on Wednesday night at 6:30 PM and visitation on Thursday night. The fourth Sunday you will teach Mr. Smith's class. The Wednesday after you have taught I will ask you how you feel about working with that age group and answer any other questions you may have. You will have the option of deciding whether that is the age group with which you feel best suited to work."

The Plan:

First Week: Enlist the worker. Give the worker the study course book, *Basic Sunday School Work* (the one for the age group chosen by you or the potential worker).

Second Week: The prospective worker should be reading the book and answering the questionnaire. The worker should observe in the department, class, weekly workers' meeting, and visitation night.

Third Week: Again, the prospective worker should observe

in the department, class, weekly workers' meeting and visitation night.

Fourth Week: The prospective worker should teach the lesson, and attend the weekly workers' meeting and visitation.

Fifth Week: The prospective worker should meet with the leader for discussion of his attitude and feelings about working with that age group. He should be given an option for decision on how he feels about that age group, spiritually, educationally, emotionally, and physically. If the prospective worker says, "Working with adults is not for me," the leader may ask, "Which age group would you prefer, youth or children?" Don't let the prospective worker off the "hook." Remember, the Lord led you to him as a worker.

When another age group is chosen, the prospective worker goes through the same process again for another five weeks with the new age group he has chosen. If necessary, stay with the prospective worker for twenty weeks until he has been exposed to every age group and has found a place of service in the Sunday School. If he has not found his place by then, make him a general officer! I know you are laughing at that line, but all joking aside, he probably is the most qualified person to be a general officer. He has read the books for every age group and had exposure of working with each age group of the entire Sunday School. Probably none of your present general officers have had that much experience or training. The real purpose, however, is to help the prospective worker enlisted to find the most suitable place to work emotionally, physically, educationally, and spiritually. Using this method you have prepared a worker for life.

The person will probably continue as a worker longer than one who has had a quarterly shoved into his hands and been told to go teach Sunday School next Sunday. The reason is that he has had a better foundation before teaching. Usually, in the "shove" method, a worker fails, quits, and is lost for life. The next time he is approached to be a worker he will say, "I tried once and failed. I just can't teach."

This approach does several things for the prospective worker: It gives a foundation of knowledge about the age group he is about to work with. It allows him to learn by observing what goes on in a department or class, learning techniques that are used in teaching, observing attitudes and actions of that age group. It allows a prospective worker to experience and actually work with an age group without the responsibility of being a full-time worker. The prospective worker experiences the helps he will receive in planning at workers' meetings. They find out what visitation is like. It gives the prospective worker the option of finding the age group he is best suited to work with.

After a person has gone through the five-week training program, he continues his training in home study of the other books for that age group. He continues to learn by taking part in the periodic study courses offered by the church or association.

There are several long-range teacher-training programs where new workers can become involved. Plan an annual calendar, leading all workers to acquire the "Sunday School Leadership Diploma." Order free leaflets, *Training Sunday School Workers* from your state Sunday School office. The leaflet lists the required books for each age group and general officer diploma. Note that three of the books, *Basic Sunday School Work*, *The Baptist Faith and Message*, and *An Introduction to the Bible* are required for every age group. Therefore, it is wise to consider having classes at times when most of the workers can attend. The following schedule is a suggestion. Start the emphasis the first Sunday of a quarter.

For eight to thirteen weeks, use the book *Basic Sunday School Work*. The number of weeks can be decided by the leader, depending upon how much time he wants to spend on each chapter or subject area. The leader for this class could be the pastor, the minister of education, Sunday School director, or some other qualified worker.

The Sunday evening worship hour may be used for eight to thirteen weeks to teach the book *The Baptist Faith and Message* by Hobbs. The number of weeks can be determined by the leader, depending upon how much time he wants to spend on each chapter or subject area. The leader would probably be the pastor. Congregations certainly need all the help they can get in Baptist faith and doctrine. This also helps the preacher to preach a distinctive series of sermons.

The Wednesday night prayer meeting hour or another series of Sunday nights for eight to thirteen weeks may be used to teach the book *An Introduction to the Bible* by L. D. Johnson. The number of weeks can be decided by the leader depending on how much time he wants to spend on each chapter or subject area. The leader would probably be the pastor.

For thirteen weeks, thirty minutes during the weekly workers' meeting could be used for teaching the *Basic* age-group books for each age group. Four *Basic* age-group books could be taught simultaneously. The leader would probably be the age-group coordinator or a worker in the age group. A chapter each week could be taught. A book could be taught each quarter. Another option is that a Saturday from 9:00 AM to 3:00 PM could be used for the teaching of one of the required age-group books. Two Saturdays out of each quarter could be devoted to the additional books.

Smaller churches could use the home study method for their required age-group books, where there are only a few, or one worker for each age group.

Another option for the small church that has only two workers for an age group is that the workers could meet on Wednesday night. One worker could read the chapter aloud to the others in their class or department room. They could talk about the suggestions the book gives as they read along and apply the suggestions. The next week the other worker could read the next chapter aloud to the other worker. This could be done week after week until the book is completed. A "high-powered," stepped-up training approach is also possible. It is possible to train every worker in the church and have them receive their workers' diplomas at the end of one quarter. I personally would not try that but would calendar the training over a nine month to a year period. For sure, set a graduation date, June or January, and calendar accordingly.

Remember, many people respond to a challenge. To those workers who could not attend the training schedule of one of the books, encouragement should be given to use home study methods like the one outlined at the beginning of this article.

The above schedule would indicate a pastor's interest in Sunday School and priority on training workers. The reason for a pastor's heavy involvement is that he is probably the best qualified, most positive teacher in the church. People will generally follow the pastor and do what he wants done.

This approach will give increased attendance in Church Training, Sunday evening worship services, and Wednesday night activities.

This schedule takes advantage of a congregation's most available time for attendance. This takes the best advantage of the church's "energy crunch."

A pastor will receive the assurance that he is training present and potential workers. He will also be teaching and training other members of the congregation in biblical history, background, and in Baptist doctrinal faith and message, using *The Baptist Faith and Message* and *An Introduction to the Bible.* This method of preaching/teaching will give him a closer relationship to his congregation.

Second Peter 3:18 says we are to "grow in grace, and in the knowledge of our Lord and Saviour, Jesus Christ." The above schedule can be adapted in a number of ways by spreading the teaching of each book throughout the year.

Basic Sunday School Work
by Harry Piland

Personal Learning Activities *

Chapter 1

1. Identify a word or phrase to describe or illustrate each of the five concepts embodied in the nature of the church._____

_____

_____

_____

_____

2. How would you define the mission of the church? What is the importance of the Bible in understanding the mission of the church?_____

_____

_____

_____

3. The writer says, "Our mission is for Christ, in love, and to persons." To see persons as Jesus saw them, what do you think Christian leaders must do to respond in love?_____

_____

_____

_____

4. Look over the reasons that the Sunday School is well-equipped to serve as a major outreach organization of the church. Identify at least one reason where you and your church may need to give more attention._____

_____

_____

Chapter 2

1. Indicate one significant contribution or happening each for the Flake, Barnette, Washburn periods in the historical roots of the Sunday School movement._____

_____

_____

2. Look at the tasks of the Sunday School. For each task, suggest a word or phrase that interprets the work of the Sunday School._____

_____

_____

_____

3. In fifty words or less, paraphrase Harry Piland's vision. What is your vision of what can happen in your church through its Sunday School?_____

_____

_____

_____

_____

Chapter 3

1. List some reasons for having organization in the Sunday School._____

_____

_____

_____

2. What are the major structures through which Sunday School work is done?_____

_____

_____

_____

3. What are three suggested guidelines for each of the four age divisions in organizing Sunday School work?_____

_____

_____

_____

_____

4. What are some ways to use records?_____

_____

_____

_____

5. Why is the pastor the key to effective organization?_____

_____

_____

_____

6. How do you respond personally to values of annual promotion as listed in this chapter? Identify one positive and one negative response._____

_____

_____

_____

7. Look at the guidelines for considering organization

options. With your type situation (small, middle-sized, large, inner-city, mission) in mind, list those that seem similar to your situation._____

_____

_____

8. What is the timeless formula for Sunday School organization?_____

_____

_____

Chapter 4

1. How do you feel about the qualities and characteristics of a Sunday School leader? In your opinion, which of the characteristics is most often overlooked in worker enlistment? Why?_____

_____

2. In the section or sections related to your job assignments, name at least two of your responsibilities._____

_____

_____

3. What are the major sources for compiling and listing

potential workers? What are your suggestions for using the series of questions about each church member?_____

_____

_____

4. List some ideas to develop motivation within persons. From your list, explain how one approach was used effectively with you by another leader._____

_____

_____

_____

_____

5. Check the requirements for credit on a Sunday School Leadership Diploma. Since this is one of the required books, when do you expect to receive your diploma?_____

_____

Chapter 5

1. Several groups are identified as planning groups. Describe one thing that actually happens in each one._____

_____

_____

_____

_____

2. What are some ways standards can be used by the Sunday School, by departments, and by classes?_____

_____

_____

_____

3. Prepare a list of ways plans are communicated. Circle those that are used in your church._____

_____

_____

_____

_____

Chapter 6

1. Dr. Piland suggests that solid weekly workers' meetings will produce better teachers and greater successes in reaching people. Do you agree? disagree? Why?_____

_____

_____

2. Outline the steps general officers should take to begin weekly workers' meetings._____

_____

_____

3. If you are from a small Sunday School, what are some suggestions for conducting the meeting in small Sunday Schools?_____

_____

_____

_____

4. Identify two things that actually happen:
   a. In the department directors' period.

   _____

   _____

   b. In the general period.

   _____

   _____

   c. In the department period—administering department concerns.

   _____

d. In the department period—planning for teaching-learning.

_____

_____

_____

_____

Chapter 7

1. Identify some biblical references to reaching. Which passage has a particular tug at your heart? Why?_____

_____

_____

2. List groups of special people your church should attempt to reach. Check those for which some provision is made in your church. Circle those where no provision presently exists for persons with special needs. Investigate further one of those circled about what possibly could be done by the beginning of the new church year._____

_____

_____

3. What responsibility do Sunday School workers and members have in visiting, contacting, and enrolling prospects?_

_____

_____

Chapter 8

1. Prepare a chart with headings as shown. Look through the chapter and insert appropriate words and phrases in the two columns.

	NEEDS	HOW LEARNED
Preschoolers		
Children		
Youth		
Adult		

2. What, if anything, impressed you about the basic guidelines followed by persons who design Sunday School Bible study materials?_____

_____

3. What one new thought surfaced from your reading the age-group suggestions under "Teaching Requires the Proper

Setting"?_____

_____

Chapter 9

1. Select one New Testament example of a verbal witness. Write a brief, first-person monologue or statement of what the early witness probably said and felt._____

_____

_____

_____

_____

_____

2. List some ways in which churches can sensitize members to be aware of unsaved persons._____

_____

_____

_____

3. How do departments and classes offer evangelistic opportunities?_____

_____

4. In order to lead someone to Christ, what must leaders and members do beyond merely talking about Jesus or the church?_____

_____

_____

Chapter 10

1. Why is the caring or ministering task such an integral part of the Sunday School?_____

_____

2. How do Sunday School classes and departments foster fellowship?_____

_____

3. Recognizing that the Holy Spirit is our power source write out a personal prayer from you—a Sunday School leader—regarding your own Sunday School responsibility.____

_____

_____

_____

_____

*This is a sample of a questionnaire that can be made for each study course book.

Notes and Thoughts

5

Soul Winning Is Important

A Simple System to Be a Soul Winner

To many Christians a special meaning for the phrase "The Roman Road" is common knowledge. Much to my amazement, one day when leading a soul-winning workshop in South Carolina I discovered it was not familiar to many others.

There were twenty-eight Sunday School workers in the morning periods. Two of these were preachers. I asked the question, "How many of you know what the Roman Road is?"

About a dozen hands went up—one being one of the preachers. I was surprised. So I said, "Have the rest of you even heard the phrase, The Roman Road?" Several more hands went up. Not half of the group had heard the phrase, let alone knew how to use it. And these were religious leaders from churches that had an aggressive outreach emphasis and mind-set.

I pointed to one person who did not lift his hand and asked, "What did you think I meant when I said the 'Roman Road?' "

His reply was, "I thought you meant some highway in Italy." I asked another person what he thought I meant, and he said, "I thought you meant the Appian Way."

This same incident has been repeated a number of times since. Therefore, it is my opinion we as leaders have not offered this plan enough times. I feel the following plan should be presented at least once a year at the beginning of the Sunday School year to make sure each worker is equipped to present the plan of salvation regardless of how inadequate the worker may feel he is to do so.

The Roman Road

The Roman Road is a system of presenting the Scriptures for salvation, using basically one book in the New Testament —the book of Romans.

When teaching your workers to use the method, have each one bring his Bible or New Testament. Start with Romans 1:16: "For I am not ashamed of the gospel of Christ: for it is the power of God unto salvation to every one that believeth; to the Jew first, and also to the Greek." Have the workers find the verse in their Bibles and underline it. Then in the margin of the Bible have them write 3:23, the next verse to be used in presenting the plan.

A comment of explanation on verse 1:16: *When a person comes to know Christ as Savior and comes to a realization of what Christ has done for him, he is not ashamed of him, but gladly tells others of him and what he means to the Christian This becomes the reality of "Christ living in you."*

Each leader when presenting this system will add his own personal interpretation of each verse. So realize there is no attempt to do much more than present the simple concept of each verse.

The next verse is Romans 3:23: "For all have sinned, and come short of the glory of God." Have each worker underline the verse and in the margin write 6:23.

A comment of explanation: *Every person before accepting Christ must realize and accept that he is a sinner and that being a sinner he is lacking or falling short of being able to be a part of God's glory because God cannot tolerate sin.*

The next verse, Romans 6:23: "For the wages of sin is death; but the gift of God is eternal life through Jesus Christ our Lord." Each worker should underline this verse and in the margin write 5:8.

A comment of explanation: *This verse gives us the end results of being a sinner, a life of work and drudgery to be rewarded with death. God, because of his loving, forgiving nature, wants to give us a gift. A gift is free, no strings attached, not given for work, full of joy and much happiness, even better than the gifts we receive at Christmas or birthday. That gift is eternal life with God in heaven, peace, joy, happiness, light, love, and all the good things we know in this life and more. To receive that gift, we must accept Jesus Christ as Savior.*

The next verse is Romans 5:8: "But God commendeth his love toward us, in that while we were yet sinners, Christ died for us." Each worker should underline the verse and write 10:9,10.

A comment of explanation: *God loved us so much that though we were sinners, he allowed his Son Jesus to be crucified on a cross so our sins might be forgiven. Jesus became the sacrifice for our sins. We are to accept the fact that God did this for us.*

The next verses are Romans 10:9,10: "That if thou shalt confess with thy mouth the Lord Jesus, and shalt believe in thine heart that God hath raised him from the dead, thou shalt be saved. For with the heart man believeth unto righteousness; and with the mouth confession is made unto salvation." Each worker should underline the verse and in the margin write John 10:28. (I leave the book of Romans, and you will see why in a moment.)

A comment of explanation: *When a person accepts Christ he should confess Christ openly and publicly. He must believe in his whole being that God did send his Son to the cross, that God did raise him from the dead, and that God can and will*

*give eternal life to those who confess with their mouths and
believe in their hearts. Upon confessing with your mouth and
believing in your heart, God gives you that gift of eternal life.*

At this place in soul-winning system of presenting the plan
of salvation, I ask the person if he would like to accept Christ
now, to take me by the hand, pray a prayer for forgiveness
and of acceptance of Christ.

I do this physical thing of taking the person by the hand because it is an outward manifestation of an inward decision. I
pray a prayer in short phrases and have the person making the
decision repeat each phrase after me. This I believe is fulfilling
the part of 10:9,10 that refers to confessing with thy mouth."

The prayer is something like this: "Dear Lord, (person being
led to the Lord repeats) I know I'm a sinner (repeat) because
your Word tells me so (repeat). Forgive me of my sins (repeat). I accept you as my Savior (repeat). I'm confessing with
my mouth (repeat). I'm believing in my heart (repeat) that
God raised Jesus from the dead (repeat). Thank you Jesus
(repeat) for saving my soul (repeat). In Jesus' name I pray
(repeat). Amen (repeat)."

I then ask, "Do you believe Jesus saved you?" The response is yes. How do you know? The general answer is "Because I asked him to and I believed in my heart."

Now ask your workers to turn to John 10:28, "And I give
unto them eternal life; and they shall never perish, neither
shall any man pluck them out of my hand." Each worker
should underline the verse and in the margin write 1 John 1:9.

A comment of explanation: *Many times, after conversion,
because of circumstances, physical feelings, things said or
done, a person's conscience will begin to bother him, to the
point he may think he is not saved, and never really was because a Christian wouldn't do, act, say, or feel the way he
does.*

The new Christian must realize that once God accepts a per-

son and the person becomes a born-again believer, he is
always saved, forever and forever.

No man, situation, or thing can take that person out of the
hand of God. This gives the individual the security of the believer. He cannot be saved today and lost tomorrow.

I feel that this is a very important step in the total plan of
salvation. I believe it is especially necessary when dealing with
older children and youth. They have such a vast number of
traumatic experiences growing into adulthood: physical, emotional, educational, financial, and experimental to find their
direction in life. Sometimes they find themselves in a situation
that causes them to think a Christian wouldn't do what they
are doing and to conclude that they must not be saved.

The new convert should be made aware of the security of
the believer. He should be told that when he commits sin, he
should ask forgiveness, and God will forgive (1 John 1:9).

Now ask your worker to turn to 1 John 1:9: "If we confess
our sins, he is faithful and just to forgive us our sins, and to
cleanse us from all unrighteousness."

Comment of explanation: *When we knowingly have com-*
mitted a wrong before God, at that moment, wherever we
are, prayer can be made with eyes open — walking, riding, sit-
ting or wherever. Confess the wrong and ask God to forgive
you and help you not to commit the same wrong again.

The above is a simple system of leading your workers to
have at their fingertips a plan of salvation available to them so
when a person might ask, "How can I be saved or born
again?" an answer can be given. It will also cause the worker
to be more conscious of presenting the plan of salvation because he knows he has a plan to present.

It has been my feeling for a long time that we have compli-
cated the plan of salvation. Unknowingly we as leaders have
left an impression that only a few, highly-trained, skilled individuals can be soul-winners. This has come about by having a
number of soul-winning classes for special groups to memorize

certain Scriptures to deal with certain individuals and situations. An impression is left that to be an effective witness, one needs to know a hundred Scriptures. Sometimes it doesn't leave much room for the work of the Holy Spirit.

"A Child Shall Lead Them"

As a minister of education a practice I had was to visit a child in our Sunday School when he became nine or ten years old. I would make an appointment with the parents to come by their home to present the plan of salvation (Roman Road above) to their child in their presence.

When I would arrive and pass the various necessary amenities I would ask the child to bring his Bible. I would ask the parent if it was acceptable to them if we marked the child's Bible. Now this is a necessary point, for some people have a thing about marking the Bible. So this is a courtesy question. If the parents did have reservations, I carried a New Testament for that person to mark and leave with them. Most people have no problem at this point. Also I have discovered sometimes there is no Bible or New Testament in the house.

I go to the house for several reasons, which you will see in a moment. One reason is I want the parent to see, hear, and feel the atmosphere and methods that are being used. I don't want a parent to feel his child was coerced or manipulated.

Another reason is that I generally knew what the spiritual state of the parents was, whether they were lost, needed to move a letter, or to rededicate a life. In the home after a spiritual experience with their child, the door is generally open to deal with the parents. I would turn to the parents and say (if they were lost), "Say, Dad, Mom, what about you? Wouldn't you like to accept Jesus Christ also and make the family complete? If you would, take my hand and let's pray the same prayer as your child."

Or, if the parents were Baptists and needed to move a letter, I suggested they do so Sunday and make the family complete in the church.

In some instances, if they were members of the church, I suggested they walk the aisle for rededication as a total family together in commitment to God's will.

A third reason is that in the presentation if I felt the child was not spiritually ready to accept Christ, I didn't lead them into making a decision at Romans 10:9,10, but stopped there and told the parent I didn't believe the child was ready and that I would come back at a later date.

There is no concrete method or test. I have come to the above conclusion only through praying for the leadership of the Holy Spirit to so sensitize me to be aware of when to stop. I am not so much seeking members, but seeking the spiritual wholeness of people.

Carry a Church Membership Card

When going into the homes, carry church membership cards in your pocket or Bible. After persons have accepted Christ, *fill out the membership card* in the home. Talk to them about walking the aisle and presenting themselves as a candidate for baptism Sunday or transfer of letter. Give them the card to place in their Bibles. This way when Sunday comes and they walk the aisle, all questions are asked and answered in a relaxed setting. The card is filled out completely. All that is needed is to hand the card to the person receiving down front.

The filled-out card in the Bible becomes a motivator for the person to be at church Sunday. It motivates the persons to step out on the first stanza. It creates an air of expectancy.

I had a person tell me he was so happy this was done in the home because he had such a fear of going down front and answering questions he might not know the answers to.

Consequently, he had stood back for months out of fear.

So, in the home, fill out the cards for those accepting Christ, transferring a letter, or those rededicating their lives and family to greater commitment for the Lord.

Be a card-carrying leader!

More Scriptures for Soul-Winners

The Word of God is used by the Holy Spirit to bring conviction and faith to the hearts of unsaved men and women. Here are some choice verses for witnessing.

The unsaved sinner must realize his spiritual condition. These verses will help him to know that he is a sinner and that he is lost.

Romans 3:10:

"As it is written, There is none righteous, no, not one."

Romans 3:23:

"For all have sinned, and come short of the glory of God."

Isaiah 53:6:

"All we like sheep have gone astray; we have turned every one to his own way; and the Lord hath laid on him the iniquity of us all."

Jeremiah 17:9:

"The heart is deceitful above all things, and desperately wicked: who can know it?"

Ephesians 2:1:

"And you hath he quickened, who were dead in trespasses and sins."

Ephesians 2:12:

"That at that time ye were without Christ, being aliens from the commonwealth of Israel, and strangers from the covenants of promise, having no hope, and without God in the world."

Revelation 20:15:

"And whosoever was not found written in the book of life was cast into the lake of fire."

Romans 6:23:

"For the wages of sin is death; but the gift of God is eternal life through Jesus Christ our Lord."

The unsaved person must realize that salvation has been provided in Christ.

John 3:16:

"For God so loved the world, that he gave his only begotten Son: that whosoever believeth in him should not perish, but have everlasting life."

1 Timothy 1:15:

"This is a faithful saying, and worthy of all acceptation, that Christ Jesus came into the world to save sinners; of whom I am chief."

John 3:17:

"For God sent not his Son into the world to condemn the world; but that the world through him might be saved."

Romans 5:8:

"But God commendeth his love toward us, in that, while we were yet sinners, Christ died for us."

John 1:29:

"The next day John seeth Jesus coming unto him, and saith, Behold the Lamb of God, which taketh away the sin of the world."

Isaiah 53:5:

"But he was wounded for our transgressions, he was bruised for our iniquities: the chastisement of our peace was upon him; and with his stripes we are healed."

2 Corinthians 5:21:

"For he hath made him to be sin for us, who knew no sin; that we might be made the righteousness of God in him."

The individual must know that he can be saved through re-

pentance and faith in Christ, and he should profess his faith.
John 3:18:

"He that believeth on him is not condemned: but he that believeth not is condemned already, because he hath not believed in the name of the only begotten Son of God."

John 3:36:

"He that believeth on the Son hath everlasting life: and he that believeth not the Son shall not see life; but the wrath of God abideth on him."

Luke 13:3:

"Except ye repent, ye shall all likewise perish."

Proverbs 29:1:

"He, that being often reproved hardeneth his neck, shall suddenly be destroyed, and that without remedy."

Acts 16:31:

"And they said, Believe on the Lord Jesus Christ, and thou shalt be saved, and thy house."

John 1:12:

"But as many as received him, to them gave he power to become the sons of God, even to them that believe on his name."

Ephesians 2:8,9:

"For by grace are ye saved through faith; and that not of yourselves: it is the gift of God. Not of works, lest any man should boast."

Romans 10:9,10:

"That if thou shalt confess with thy mouth the Lord Jesus and shalt believe in thine heart that God hath raised him from the dead, thou shalt be saved. For with the heart man believeth unto righteousness; and with the mouth confession is made unto salvation."

Matthew 10:32,33:

"Whosoever therefore shall confess me before men, him will I confess also before my Father which is in heaven. But

whosoever shall deny me before men, him will I also deny before my Father which is in heaven."
Isaiah 1:18:

"Come now, and let us reason together, saith the Lord: though your sins be as scarlet, they shall be as white as snow; though they be red like crimson, they shall be as wool."
Isaiah 55:7:

"Let the wicked forsake his way, and the unrighteous man his thoughts: and let him return unto the Lord, and he will have mercy upon him; and to our God, for he will abundantly pardon."

Notes and Thoughts

Scriptures Used in This Book

Ephesians 3:20: "Now unto him that is able to do exceeding abundantly above all that we ask or think, according to the power that worketh in us."

Proverbs 23:7: "For as he thinketh in his heart, so is he: Eat and drink, saith he to thee; but his heart is not with thee."

1 Peter 2:2: "As newborn babes, desire the sincere milk of the word, that ye may grow thereby."

James 4:17: "Therefore to him that knoweth to do good, and doeth it not, to him it is sin."

2 Peter 3:18: "But grow in grace, and in the knowledge of our Lord and Saviour Jesus Christ. To him be glory both now and for ever."

Colossians 3:2: "Set your affection on things above, not on things on the earth."

Matthew 15:18: "But those things which proceed out of the mouth come forth from the heart; and they defile the man."

Matthew 7:20: "Wherefore by their fruits ye shall know them."

James 4:2b: "Ye have not, because ye ask not."

2 Timothy 2:15: "Study to shew thyself approved unto God, a workman that needeth not to be ashamed, rightly dividing the word of truth."

Matthew 25:21a: "His lord said unto him, Well done, thou good and faithful servant."

1 Corinthians 9:22b: "I am made all things to all men, that I might by all means save some."

Psalm 37:7a: "Rest in the Lord."

Psalm 34:8: "O taste and see that the Lord is good: blessed is the man that trusteth in him."

John 4:13: "Jesus answered and said unto her, Whosoever drinketh of this water shall thirst again."

Proverbs 28:25b: "He that putteth his trust in the Lord shall be made fat."

Revelation 3:20: "Behold, I stand at the door, and knock: if any man hear my voice, and open the door, I will come in to him, and will sup with him, and he with me."

Proverbs 22:6: "Train up a child in the way he should go: and when he is old, he will not depart from it."

Luke 14:23: "And the lord said unto the servant, Go out into the highways and hedges, and compel them to come in, that my house may be filled."

Romans 10:14: "How then shall they call on him in whom they have not believed? and how shall they believe in him of whom they have not heard? and how shall they hear without a preacher?"

Psalm 37:5: "Commit thy way unto the Lord; trust also in him; and he shall bring it to pass."

Proverbs 3:5,6: "Trust in the Lord with all thine heart; and lean not unto thine own understanding. In all thy ways acknowledge him, and he shall direct thy paths."

2 Kings 21:13b: "As a man wipeth a dish, wiping it, and turning it upside down."

Notes and Thoughts